GROW WILD!

GROW WILD!

NATIVE-PLANT
GARDENING IN CANADA
AND NORTHERN UNITED STATES

LORRAINE JOHNSON

PHOTOGRAPHS BY ANDREW LEYERLE

RANDOM HOUSE OF CANADA

A DENISE SCHON BOOK

A Denise Schon Book

Published in the United States of America by Fulcrum Publishing

Canadian Cataloguing in Publication Data

Johnson, Lorraine
　　　Grow wild!: native plant gardening in Canada and northern United States

ISBN 0-679-30919-5

1. Native plant gardening – Canada.　　2. Plants, Ornamental – Canada.　I. Title

SB439.26.C3J625 1998　635.9'5171　　　　C97-932276-6

The author has tried to be as accurate as possible with information supplied by
gardeners and acknowledged authorities. We regret any errors or omissions.

Design: Counterpunch/Linda Gustafson
Editor: Jennifer Glossop
Production: Counterpunch and Bookmaker's Press Inc.
Production co-ordination: Anna Barron
Index and botanical fact-checking: Barbara Schon

Printed and bound in Canada by Tri-graphic Printing Ltd.

10　9　8　7　6　5　4　3　2　1

Additional photography:
Photograph on p. 71 by Larry Lamb
Photograph on p. 117 by Lorraine Johnson
Photograph on p. 93 by Jim Hodgins

Table of Contents

INTRODUCTION

The dialogue between the wild and the tame is one of the essential stories our gardens tell.

EVERY GARDEN HAS a story – a narrative that unfolds as people animate the space. Every garden has a history – the triumphs and tragedies that made it what it is. And every garden has an identity – the soul of its soil, the dreams of its plantings, the eccentricities of its stewards, the vagaries of its weather, the synchronicities of its many creatures, invited by chance, invited by design.

Gardeners set these stories in motion by sowing the seeds for the kind of random dramas that bring a place to life. But however precise the planning, gardening is always about change, dynamic, shifting change – sometimes fortuitous, sometimes heartbreaking, always revealing. Every success and every failure tell us something about the garden, about the appropriateness of our inclinations, about the insistence of nature's imperatives. We can fiddle around at the edges, pushing zones, testing tolerance, but the essential fact is that nature calls the shots. No matter how assured we may be in our abilities, there's always the stray seedling that rejects our ministrations, the cardinal flower that demands to be mulched, the cardinal flower that demands *not* to be mulched.

We learn such idiosyncrasies only by doing. Luckily, however, the doings of others can contribute to our understanding, not as a substitute for our own dirty fingernails but as concentric circles that expand outward from our efforts to those of the larger community, to those similarly obsessed with the secrets and subtleties of nurtured growth.

All gardeners participate in a kind of communal exercise of shaping and reshaping, of honing and fine-tuning the landscape we share. Perhaps community is what gardening is all about: from the microcommunity of one small plot, with its botanical inhabitants rubbing crowded shoulders, to the macro-community of the larger landscape and our collective vision of how that landscape – *this* landscape of Earth – might flourish. We enact these visions and ideas – both micro and macro – every time we put trowel to dirt. And we share these visions and ideas with every gardening story we tell.

Here, then, are dozens of gardening tales, the collective wisdom of gardening novices and gardening experts. The one thing they share – besides the accumulated scrubbings of many tired and triumphant hands – is a commitment to community, the community of native-plant enthusiasts across North America, a community working hard to heal the land, garden by garden.

THE PROMISE AND POSSIBILITIES OF NATIVE-PLANT GARDENING

PICTURE A THRIVING residential community in a typical North American city. The front yards are surrounded by pavement and are covered with the botanical equivalent of pavement: lawns. And tucked up to the houses on this street are regimental plantings of the benignly familiar shrubs, maybe a lollipop-looking tree marooned like an orphan in a sea of grass, perhaps ringed with the regulation exotic shade-lovers such as hostas and periwinkle. It could be anywhere in North America.

But one yard stands out as different, offering signposts that root us in a particular place. For starters, the birds are squawking up a riot – an exuberant contrast to the silence next door, where no seedpods or berries or brush exist to lure them. And in the aural spaces between the drone of traffic, you catch a different kind of rhythm: the hum of insects, some losing the battle and becoming bird dinner, others making their way deep into flowers, drinking captured rainwater, picking up pollen.

The winged diversity of this yard has its parallel on the ground too. Instead of the handful of plant choices offered throughout the neighborhood, there are dozens of different plantings: colorful native meadow plants in the sunny center and the subdued cooling greens of shady woodlanders in the darker corners. You count 50 species, and those are just the ones immediately identifiable. A check in the field guide reveals a dozen more.

I've seen literally hundreds of such yards – the yards of native-plant gardeners, who are forging a new landscape aesthetic – and what stands out so forcefully in each one is that these places are *alive*. With life comes surprises and unplanned changes and a letting go of total control, but with life also comes diversity, a sense that there are many hands at work, many connections and interactions and creatures following their own paths, doing their own work as pieces of a complex puzzle.

All the native-plant gardeners I've met celebrate this diversity and are humble before the complexity of the puzzle. They don't presume to know all the answers; rather, they see the garden as the space of learning, of lived experience. Sure, they've discovered tricks that work, tricks that don't, tricks to share, tricks to dump. But the tricks aren't battle tactics (an all-too-familiar metaphor of conventional gardening); instead, they're the inevitable tricks of partnership, the give and take of negotiated alliance.

Above all, the alliance forged in native-plant gardening is with nature – nature as teacher, guide and eventually, as our knowledge expands, partner.

Previous spread: Though spring ephemeral plants such as trilliums go dormant in summer, careful planning will ensure that foliage plants such as ferns will fill in any gaps.

NATIVE-PLANT GARDENING is a landscape trend that has explosively taken hold of North America during the past decade or so. Where I live, in Toronto, Ontario, you would have been hard-pressed five years ago to find many sources of native plants in the regular nursery trade; now, it's almost a chic necessity for garden centers to display special sections of native offerings.

This newfound interest transcends the regular story of market forces, the dreary tale of commercial supply and demand, and speaks instead to a radical shift in the way we think about our gardens, our landscapes and, indeed, the planet as a whole. Gone – or at least severely stressed – are the days of blinkered disconnection, when we believed that our interactions with the Earth had no consequences. The realization is growing that every intervention has an impact and that for too long, our impact has harmed rather than healed the land on which we depend for everything from bodily nourishment to spiritual sustenance.

How might our landscape interventions be more positive, how might they restore the land to health rather than participate in its ongoing decline? Native-plant gardening offers at least one answer to this crucial question. And it's an answer that is available to all of us with gardens to tinker in, land to steward. You don't need acres and acres of "pristine" wilderness to have a positive impact; indeed, it's probably in those areas most stressed by urban pressures – denuded, defoliated and in decline – that we can make the biggest difference.

By gardening with native plants, you're taking a giant leap toward ecological balance. To begin with, you'll be using a lot less water. Even if you don't live in an area with depleted watertables, water restrictions are a familiar fact of life in many North American communities. Quite simply, we waste too much of the stuff, and each wasted drop represents wasted energy and wasted resources – the accumulated pumping, processing, cleansing and delivering of our infrastructure systems.

Native plants are adapted to the natural water regimes of the area. Compared with exotic plants, natives require much less in the way of supplementary watering. Sure, if you've planted moisture-loving woodlanders such as Jack-in-the-pulpits and mayapples under the drying canopy and Hooverish root

The Wild Ones, a nonprofit group of natural landscapers, has a succinct definition that captures the spirit of native-plant gardening:

"Natural landscaping is more beneficial than toxic (choosing organic methods over poisonous ones); more enlightened than trendy (reviving ecosystems rather than planting indiscriminately); more joyous than tedious (growing ever-changing plantscapes instead of mow-me-every-week turf grass)."

Source: *Wild Ones Handbook* (Milwaukee: The Wild Ones, 1997).

systems of the ubiquitous nonnative Norway maple, you'll need to water; but if you've carefully matched the natives to the conditions – trying, for example, the forgiving and merrily multiplying Canada violet – you'll use much less water. Certainly a lot less than the 10,000 gallons (38,000 L) demanded by the average 25-by-40-foot (7.5 m x 12 m) lawn each summer.

Then there's the contentious issue of herbicide and pesticide use. On that score, too, native-plant gardens come out ahead. While other gardeners line up on both sides of the debate, native-plant gardeners find that the issue seldom arises. With their diverse and ecologically balanced gardens, pest problems are rarely catastrophic and simply don't require drastic chemical measures on an ongoing basis. A spray bottle of soap and water, eternal weed vigilance and a strong back are the required tools. (And a curiosity about how long it will take the ladybugs to consume the aphid infestation.) The majority of native-plant gardeners I've encountered don't do much in the way of pest enforcement, adopting instead a live-and-let-live attitude, with little in the way of visible damage to show for it. I conclude, therefore, that most native-plant gardeners are organic gardeners, whether by intention or by default, and that such an approach serves them well.

Not all visiting creatures are of the sort reviled in the chemical-company literature, of course. Recently, there's been quite an upsurge of interest in "theme" gardens that attract butterflies or hummingbirds or other creatures. I chuckle each time a nursery catalog offers such kits. Quite simply, if you want to attract native butterflies and birds to your garden, spend your pennies on native plants, not on contraptions and potions. Plants and animals have evolved together over thousands of years; chances are that if you plant the natives, the creatures will find you.

So far, this enumeration of benefits has been of things you can point to and celebrate. To my mind, however, the most important benefit of native-plant gardening is intangible (and verging on inarticulate): the way that native-plant gardening connects you – vitally, deeply – with the local specific environment you inhabit. You learn the plants and creatures that call the place home. You learn the rainfall patterns and microclimate details that make the place like no other. You learn the smell and texture (and maybe even taste) of the soil, the force of the wind, the clarity or moodiness of the light – in short, all the quirky, heartening, maddening specificities of place that characterize it as *this* place, not *anyplace*.

One of my favorite spring rituals is to go to a nearby woods to see the moisture-loving skunk cabbage send up its bizarre and fascinating hooded flowers. In a large garden, this plant can be used to advantage in what would otherwise be a problem area – moist, mucky, flooded ground.

We've got more than enough *anyplaces* already – a trip to the strip-mall developments surrounding most North American cities will attest to this. What we need are more landscapes, more gardens, that truly reflect the variety and vitality of each community's character – and by community, I mean not just the human inhabitants but the communities of plants and animals which contribute so much to our sense of identity, our sense of where exactly it is that we call home.

With native-plant gardening, we become what the bioregional philosophers call dwellers in the land – partners, not parasites; participants, not parallel players; dwellers, not dictators.

LIKE THE REAL ESTATE agent's mantra of "location, location, location," the question of the territory covered by this book hovered around the edges of my thinking from start to finish. How to cover the whole continent? Impossible. Restrict it to Canada and the northern regions of the United States? Much more sensible.

BENEFITS OF NATIVE-PLANT GARDENING

- Because native plants are adapted to an area, the gardener does not need to depend on an arsenal of inputs – chemical, water or otherwise – but, rather, defers to the accumulated wisdom of the plants' genetic memory. Ten thousand years of adaptive skill is surely worth deferring to. In other words, unlike their exotic nonnative-garden counterparts, native plants are actually programmed, through thousands of years of evolution, to thrive in their home range and rarely require the coddling that exotics demand.
- Along with reduced water and chemical use, the native-plant garden often requires less in the way of ongoing long-term maintenance.
- Native-plant gardens celebrate regional differences of character and, as such, counter the homogenizing trend overtaking so much of North America.
- Native plants offer food and shelter to a wide array of indigenous creatures – birds, bees and butterflies, for example – all of which bring the native-plant garden to life.
- By providing a home for plant species which are losing more and more of their wild habitats, native-plant gardens contribute to biodiversity, ensuring that local gene stocks are perpetuated.
- Through close contact with native plants, the gardener learns all about natural processes, not as some kind of theoretical construct, but as lived experience, right at one's fingertips.
- Last, but not least, native plants are beautiful!

But almost immediately, the boundaries loosened, the borders shifted, the inconsistencies escalated. How to rationalize the broad-band clumping of those marvelously and intricately distinct regions of the Northwest into the inelegantly vague and lumpy label "The Northwest"? How to acknowledge the tremendous variation between tallgrass, mixed-grass and shortgrass landscapes in a chapter called "The Prairies"? How to escape heresy in a seemingly too tidily tightened chapter on one *huge* territory of Great Lakes, Northeast, mid-Atlantic and eastern Canada titled, for the sake of convenience, "The Northeast"?

In some ways, the alliances *are* arbitrary – someone else would, by definition, draw a different map, frame a different focus. But when one sheds political boundaries, when one begins to think in terms of ecological regions instead, the map of Canada and the northern United States takes on an altogether altered shape. The 49th Parallel all but disappears. Habitat bands, like the seeping fingers of some massive hand, spread north and south, east and west, merrily scoffing at political distinctions drawn on maps. The regions drip and ooze in untidy abandon. Just when you think you've got southern Ontario pegged (Great Lakes forest), that exquisite corner of tallgrass prairie peeking into the province in the southwest surprises you.

And each of those corners, those pockets, those variations, can be further broken down into regions with increasingly specific labels. Tallgrass prairie in southwestern Ontario, for example, may be dry prairie, dry-mesic, mesic sandy loam, wet-mesic, wet-mesic sandy, wet-mesic sandy loam or wet prairie. As one delves deeper, the variations explode in logarithmic profusion.

One book can never do justice to the unimaginably complex variations at work in any one region, whatever the label. So think of the generalizations at work in this book – the labels of Northwest, Prairies, Great Lakes, Northeast, mid-Atlantic and eastern Canada – as a kind of overlay map. For the necessarily specific knowledge of your local region, you'll need to explore, interrogate, investigate and tease out the compelling logic of your home place, wherever that is in Canada or the northern regions of the United States. And, in the course of your investigations, I guarantee you'll discover that a whole book could be written about the complex quirks of each and every backyard in North America, about the specific eccentricities, challenges and triumphs of each of our home places.

Defining Native

I'll admit that my love for native-plant gardening borders on obsession. I even enjoy the spirited debates about what counts as a native plant that seem to crop up whenever one starts talking about the subject. These discussions seem to follow a predictable pattern, to wit:

Q: What's a native plant?

A: A plant that existed in a particular region prior to European settlement.

Q: Why pick the point of first contact? Isn't that arbitrary and possibly even naive, ignoring, as it does, the enormous impact that native peoples had on the land before the Europeans arrived?

A: Yes, the native peoples had an enormous impact on the land, but that pales in comparison to the wholesale and widespread alterations effected by European settlement. It was at the point of first contact and then in increasing increments thereafter that the botanical makeup of the North American continent changed massively (perhaps irrevocably) due to the deliberate or accidental introduction of exotic alien species, the suppression of such natural processes as fire, the unparalleled destruction of wilderness areas, such as forests, wetlands and prairies, the alteration of ecosystem support systems, such as the air and hydrological cycles, and the conversion of wild areas to settled, cultivated landscapes.

Q: Okay, I'll admit that human beings have done a lot of damage, but the use of terms such as "exotic" and "alien" is unsettling. We're a continent of immigrants; only the native peoples are in fact native to this land, and even they arrived thousands of years ago from another place. So why call plants such as Queen Anne's lace and dandelion, which have been here for hundreds of years, exotic or alien? Isn't this a form of botanical racism?

A: It's a simple ecological fact that some plants have evolved over thousands of years in a particular place, adapting their life processes, needs and requirements to be in sync with the ecological factors and conditions of that particular place. Equally, it's a simple ecological fact that other plants have been introduced by human actions into a place which is not their indigenous habitat. Some of these introduced plants, these "aliens" and "exotics," kick the bucket, unadapted as they are to this climate and these conditions; others give a good kick at the can but die in the long run; and still others kick up their heels and "take over" indigenous habitats, crowding out and outcompeting native species, altering the habitat in ways we are only beginning to understand.

Just how much "experimenting" (the wrong word, really, since in scientific experiments, there are *controls*) do we want to do before we admit that maybe 10,000 years of evolution are worth listening to? How many purple loosestrife infestations and Dutch elm diseases and zebra mussel debacles do we intend to put this planet through?

All this is not to say that nonnatives, exotics, aliens or whatever you want to call introduced plants do not have a rightful place in the landscapes and gardens of North America. After all, where would we be without the hundreds of nonnative food plants that grow by the thousands of acres on this continent? And where would we be without the many delightful exotics that gardeners everywhere cherish in their plots?

To embrace native-plant gardening does not necessitate botanical banishment of all nonnative species, since they certainly have their place. But native-plant proponents are attempting to reclaim a place for indigenous vegetation in our gardens and landscapes, because for too long, we have banished the native species beyond the garden gate.

FROM LUSH COASTAL FORESTS TO DRY GRASSLANDS

"THEY'RE SO LUCKY out there" is a familiar refrain when central and eastern gardeners refer to the West Coast. It's as if Westerners are somehow cheating by living in a place temperate of climate, rich in rainfall, calm of pace, blessed in diverse flora and high of zone. (And, we Easterners neglect to mention – or rub it in, depending on mood – deficient in sunlight.) Without doubt, North America's West Coast is a gardener's dream.

Nevertheless, I find myself off balance, gardening-wise, whenever I visit. As a southern Ontarian, someone usually surrounded by concrete, I can't imagine being distracted by cultivated gardens while encircled by nature's grand garden at every turn.

Luckily, West Coast gardeners don't seem to have this problem. They know the rainforest or the Garry oak meadow or the mountain wildflowers are right there, *and* they garden like mad. Indeed, many are working zealously to bring these native habitats and gardens together.

And it's not just a coastal phenomenon. In community after community in the Northwest, I was introduced to people and projects that warmed the heart (and fueled my envy): kids in Victoria, British Columbia, planting Garry oak meadow species in their schoolyard, learning all about the botanical and cultural history of their region, proudly nurturing their young gardens so that in 20 years, the next generation of pupils could spend recess in floral splendor; a garden club in Tacoma, Washington, creating a showpiece public garden, composed entirely of native species so that visitors to the region could see the beauty of the indigenous flora, feel, even if just briefly, the tug of the towering trees and imagine what the early inhabitants of the region saw; volunteers in King County, Washington, involved in a project called Habitat Partners that looks after habitat-restoration sites; a local community group in Mosier, Oregon, planting the highway verge with native meadow species, reclaiming barren, wasted space and making it bloom again.

As I soaked up the enthusiasm of the native-plant gardeners I met and the rich diversity of the region, I speculated more than once that having such beauty so close must make people truly value it, nurture it, engage with it.

Previous page: Every native-plant garden is unique, and each path leads one to rich discovery.

Diversity is, indeed, the name of the game in the Northwest. Traveling short distances, you can move through dramatic changes in climate, geography, vegetation zones and character. And with each change, a new world of plant and animal associations unfolds. One could spend an entire lifetime learning the subtle and complex tunings of nature's northwestern harmonics.

The mountains, of course, set the chord, dictating how much rain falls where, setting the stage for the various moisture regimes that control so much

of how each region has evolved, separating coast from Interior. While some areas west of the mountain ranges, for example, may receive as much as 140 inches (355 cm) of rain each year, making them some of the wettest places on the continent, other regions of the Interior make do with a paltry 12 inches (30 cm). Under such dramatically different conditions, it's no wonder that the Northwest is so rich in ecologically disparate habitats.

At the coast, the temperate rainforest looms large, with its towering conifers: Douglas fir, western hemlock, western red cedar, grand fir and Sitka spruce. Mosses, ferns and lichens drape these giants; various canopy layers create the sense of overwhelming green lushness; and the understory is rich with diverse growth. But, somewhat paradoxically, it is the forgiving fecundity of death that gives life to this forest: the masses of decaying wood on the forest floor support a complex web of species.

A burned stump, retained in the garden to attract wildlife, provides a backdrop for the rare Anderson's sword fern.

To the east are various mountain forest systems, none as lush as the coastal rainforest, but each distinctive: the ponderosa pine ecosystem, for example, with its dryness and grassland groundcovers, intergrading into the more familiar grassland communities of bunchgrass and sagebrush. As well, in British Columbia, Washington and Oregon, there are also savanna and even prairie ecosystems.

Thus the region is characterized by contrast: home to some of the largest and oldest trees on Earth, home to some of the subtlest grasslands and tiniest alpine species.

Such broad brush strokes may offer guidance, but they can't hope to encompass the specific conditions at hand in each garden. It may help to know, for example, that scientists classify the Northwest into 16 distinct natural provinces (climate zones) or that seven distinct forest regions occur in British Columbia and Washington, but what we really need to know are the quirky eccentricities that distinguish our tiny plots.

Here, for inspiration, are the stories of a few northwestern gardens: first

Perhaps no more convincing
testament to the toughness of
native plants is needed than that
reported by Don Zobel and Joseph
Antos, who excavated at the
Mount Saint Helens' site and found
two species of huckleberry, avalanche
lily and two species of moss still
alive after *87 months* of being buried
under tons of volcanic ash!

woodland, then wetland, grassland and, finally, the Garry oak meadow, one of the region's most threatened habitats. These gardeners not only have learned the details of their sites but have translated the beauty of northwestern habitats into their own gorgeous and diverse gardens.

As well, there are lists of appropriate species – woodland, wetland, grassland and Garry oak meadow – for northwestern gardeners to try. These are general lists; you'll need to determine whether a particular plant is indigenous to your specific area and appropriate for your conditions by checking a field guide or visiting wild areas in your region. However, most of the species listed have a very broad native range, and all are easy to grow.

IDENTIFYING NORTHWEST NATIVES

The most thorough source for identifying plants native to the Pacific Northwest is C. Leo Hitchcock and Arthur Cronquist's *Flora of the Pacific Northwest* (Seattle: University of Washington Press, 1973). Popular guides such as Jim Pojar and Andy MacKinnon's *Plants of the Pacific Northwest Coast* (Vancouver: Lone Pine, 1994) and *Trees, Shrubs and Flowers to Know in British Columbia and Washington* by C.P. Lyons and Bill Merilees (Vancouver: Lone Pine, 1995) also provide detailed information, as do *Plants of Southern Interior British Columbia* by Roberta Parish, Ray Coupe and Dennis Lloyd (Vancouver: Lone Pine, 1996), *Plants of Northern British Columbia* by MacKinnon et al. (Vancouver: Lone Pine, 1992), *Handbook of Northwestern Plants* by Dennis Gilkey (Portland: Oregon State University Press, 1980) and *Trees and Shrubs of British Columbia* by Christopher Brayshaw (Vancouver: University of British Columbia Press, 1996).

Field guides such as the National Audubon Society's *Field Guide to North American Wildflowers: Western Region* (New York: Knopf, 1979), Peterson's *Pacific State Wildflowers* (New York: Houghton Mifflin, 1976) and

Peterson's *Field Guide to Rocky Mountain Wildflowers* (Boston: Houghton Mifflin, 1963) are also excellent.

Other useful sources include *Wild Trees of British Columbia* by Sherman Brough (Vancouver: Pacific Educational Press, 1990), *A Field Guide to the Ecology of Western Forests* by John C. Kricher (Boston: Houghton Mifflin, 1993), *Plants and Animals of the Pacific Northwest* by Eugene Kozloff (Seattle: University of Washington Press, 1991), *The Compact Guide to Wildflowers of the Rockies* by C.D. Bush (Edmonton: Lone Pine, 1990), *Plants of the Western Boreal Forest and Aspen Parkland* by Derek Johnson (Vancouver: Lone Pine, 1996), *The Prairie Keepers* by Marcy Houle (Reading, Massachusetts: Addison-Wesley, 1996), *Wetland Plants of Oregon and Washington* by Jennifer Guard (Vancouver: Lone Pine, 1995) and *Wetland Plants of the Pacific Northwest* by Fred Weinmann et al. (Seattle: U.S. Army Corps of Engineers, 1984). A highly technical guide to plant communities is *Natural Vegetation of Oregon and Washington* by Jerry Franklin and C.T. Dyrness (Portland: Oregon State University Press, 1988).

Trees for the Northwestern Gardener

When grown in masses or clumps with an understory of sword fern, vine maple creates an enchanting woodland corner. As an added bonus, this combination requires little maintenance.

In a region in which discussions of trees and forestry often turn contentious, dividing friends, families, communities and generations, the gardener may instead retreat into the saner comfort of simply planting the things. The growth of a forest starts with a cone or seed that can be held in the palm of a hand. The unimaginable mass of a Douglas fir, for example, sequestering in its tissues 5,000 gallons (19,000 L) of water and producing 60 to 70 million seeds, all begins with a seed finding hospitable ground.

Grand fir (*Abies grandis*): With its lower branches drooping down and forming a kind of skirt, this tall conifer (approximately 125 feet/40m) is a graceful giant that often grows in association with Douglas fir. Full sun to shade; needs well-drained soil; drought-tolerant.

Bigleaf maple (*Acer macrophyllum*): Broad-leaved hardly does justice to these leaves, which can sometimes grow up to 12 inches (30 cm) across. This stately deciduous tree grows to about 100 feet (30 m), with a large spread, and produces hanging clusters of fragrant greenish yellow flowers in spring. The leaves turn yellow in fall. Shade-tolerant, but grows in moist soil in full sun.

Arbutus, a.k.a. madrone (*Arbutus menziesii*): The smooth bark of this broad-leaved evergreen gives the arbutus its most stunning landscape feature: the brownish red outer bark peels in patches to reveal the yellowish underbark. Growing about 30 to 70 feet (10–20 m) tall, the arbutus needs excellent drainage. Small, white

For the dry shade beneath Douglas fir, try planting a groundcover of bunchberry (*Cornus canadensis*), dull Oregon grape (*Mahonia nervosa*), sword fern (*Polystichum munitum*) or vanilla leaf (*Achlys triphylla*).

fragrant flowers appear in clusters in late spring; orange-red berries in fall are devoured by birds. Full sun; dry open areas.

Oregon ash (*Fraxinus latifolia*): Sometimes considered weedy and messy, this deciduous tree – the only native ash in the Northwest – nevertheless provides attractive yellow fall color, is easy to grow and reaches 80 feet (25 m). Part sun to shade; moist soil.

Pacific crab apple (*Malus fusca*, a.k.a. *Pyrus fusca*): This small tree or bushy, large multistemmed shrub grows to approximately 30 feet (9 m) and produces clusters of fragrant white flowers in spring. Its fruit is an important food source for birds, and its leaves turn yellow and red in fall. Part shade to sun; moist to dry soil.

Bitter cherry (*Prunus emarginata*): On the coast, this deciduous tree grows to approximately 50 feet (15 m), whereas in the drier Interior, it resembles a shrub. Pinkish white flowers in spring give way to bright red fruit – inedible for humans (very bitter) but important for birds. Part shade to sun; moist, well-drained soil.

Douglas fir (*Pseudotsuga menziesii*): In its coastal range, the Douglas fir grows about 230 feet (70 m) high; the Interior Douglas fir (a subspecies) is a smaller tree, stockier in shape. A fast-growing and long-lived conifer, it has a pyramidal shape, and its ease of cultivation makes it appropriate (and familiar) for landscape use. Full sun; well-drained soil.

Western red cedar (*Thuja plicata*): A familiar sight in the Northwest is the shaggy reddish bark and buttressed base of the red cedar (British Columbia's provincial tree). Growing to 200 feet (60 m), it is often sheared to form a dense hedge. Shade-tolerant; moist soil.

Western hemlock (*Tsuga heterophylla*): This shade-tolerant evergreen grows up to 200 feet (60 m) in height (with its uppermost twig and its branches drooping) and creates a dense canopy. Sun to shade; moist, well-drained, rich soil.

Woodland Shrubs for the Northwestern Gardener

Like those of almost any plant, the subtle satisfactions of shrubs can be found in the three F's: flowers, fruit and foliage. And the birds agree. It is no accident that the phrase "good for birds" is found throughout the following list. Plant these shrubs, and the birds will find you – and feast.

(Note that most of these shrubs grow naturally in open woods or forest edges; thus most are not appropriate for deeper shade. The exceptions to this, however, are vine maple and hazelnut. See page 31 for a list of sun-loving shrubs.)

Vine maple (*Acer circinatum*): A fine shade-tolerant, sprawling deciduous shrub that grows to approximately 30 feet (10 m) and turns either yellow (in shade) or red (in sun) in fall. Its showy white flowers with pinkish purple sepals appear in spring before the leaves. Sun to shade; moist soil.

Hazelnut (*Corylus cornuta*): This tall, spreading deciduous shrub (up to 12 feet/3.7 m) produces gorgeous hanging light brown catkins in late winter/early spring and edible nuts in fall. Leaves turn yellow. Shade to sun; moist, well-drained soil.

Salal (*Gaultheria shallon*): An evergreen shrub which often behaves like a groundcover, salal has glossy leaves and pinkish white flowers that hang down from stalks in spring and early summer. (My favorite description of the flower comes from Larry Lodwick, writing in *Douglasia*, the newsletter of the Washington Native Plant Society: "shaped like tiny hot-air balloons, with the opening pointed to the ground.") Purple berries in summer attract birds. Growing 3 to 6 feet (1–2 m), it can be invasive. Useful as erosion control on sand dunes, it is a tough, hardy plant. Shade to sun; dry to moist soil; drought-tolerant once established.

Tall Oregon grape (*Mahonia aquifolium*, a.k.a. *Berberis aquifolium*): With its hollylike shiny leaves and bright yellow flower clusters (the state flower of Oregon) in spring, this erect evergreen shrub is a knockout. Growing 6 to 10 feet (2–3 m), it has clusters of dark blue berries in midsummer; new foliage and winter foliage are bronzy red. Part shade to full sun on dry to moist well-drained soil; drought-tolerant. The related dull Oregon grape (*Mahonia nervosa*) thrives in shade.

Both red and blue elderberries attract birds to the garden. The red elderberry, shown here, has pyramidal flower clusters in spring and red berries in early summer; it prefers moist clearings.

Indian plum (*Oemleria cerasiformis*, a.k.a. *Osmaronia cerasiformis*): This very early-blooming deciduous shrub has whitish green, fragrant flower clusters that hang down in a graceful droop and provide a nectar source for hummingbirds. Indian plum is dioecious – it requires both a male and a female plant to set fruit. Bright orange fruits appear later in summer and ripen to dark bluish purple (they're great for birds). Leaves turn yellow in late summer. The shrub grows to approximately 12 feet (3.7 m). Deep to open shade; dry to moist soil.

Ninebark (*Physocarpus capitatus*): Small, white flower clusters in late spring look almost like little snowballs. Growing to 10 feet (3 m), this deciduous shrub does well in open woodlands. An interesting feature is the bronzy shredding bark of older branches. Full sun to open shade; moist to wet humus-rich soil.

Pacific rhododendron (*Rhododendron macrophyllum*): This large evergreen shrub (commonly to about 13 feet/ 4 m) sports showy pinkish purple flowers (the state flower of Washington) in late spring that match many of the nonnative rhodos for beauty. Add decaying wood around the base of this shrub. Part shade; well-drained, dry to moist acidic soil.

Red elderberry (*Sambucus racemosa*): Growing to 18 feet (5.5 m), this deciduous shrub has attractive, showy, fragrant, creamy white flower clusters in spring and red berries in summer, which are good for birds. It grows quickly and can be invasive. Full sun, open woodlands; well-drained sites, from dry to moist soil.

Red huckleberry (*Vaccinium parvifolium*): This erect deciduous shrub grows 3 to 13 feet (1–4 m). Spring

In the dark understory of a dense forest planting, natives such as western bleeding heart (front), wood sorrel (left and right) and Siberian miner's lettuce (middle) form a rich, lush cover.

brings pinkish yellow flowers; bright red berries in summer. Garden writer Des Kennedy offers a useful tip in the Naturescaping newsletter: If you're growing raspberries for eating, plant red huckleberry too, as the birds will eat *those* berries and leave you the raspberries. Shade to part shade; moist soil, but will also grow in sunny, drought conditions.

WINNING COMBOS FOR UNDERNEATH DRYING CONIFERS

- fringecup, inside-out flower, red huckleberry, sword fern
- inside-out flower, vanilla leaf
- false Solomon's seal, inside-out flower, trillium, vanilla leaf
- oak fern, vanilla leaf

Vanilla leaf's spreading nature can be used to advantage in the shade of a woodland garden. The carpet of leaves, with white flower spikes in spring, floats above the ground.

A Tiny Urban Forest

Vancouver, British Columbia

In the wild, broad-leaved stonecrop grows on rocky outcrops. Here, in the Skeltons' garden, it finds a home in a retaining wall. Wintergreen, with its shiny green leaves, also meanders through the rocks.

IT TOOK AN ELECTRON microscopist to teach me the lessons of small. After I had spent a few hours with Frank and Erin Skelton in their Vancouver garden and was down on all fours looking at a 4-inch-square (10 cm sq) section of moss, Frank confessed to me that he could happily devote an entire day to looking at just one cell with a microscope. I should have guessed that this scale was his passion. What I had first seen as a carpet of green was really incredibly diverse – at least three different types of club moss and a tiny seedling of volunteer Labrador tea. The lessons of small: look closely, look carefully, and look again.

Looking again and again is the compelling lure of Frank and Erin's 42-by-35-foot (13 m x 11 m) garden in Vancouver. From the moment we opened the wooden gate, we were transported to the lush world of a pond, a small waterfall and a mini urban forest, with the sound of running water punctuating the smooth calm.

In 1974, after the trauma of house renovation, Frank and Erin's front yard was a pile of scrubby fill. Gone were the privet hedge, roses and lawn that had comprised the garden when they first moved in. "We started from zero. There wasn't a native plant in the place," says Frank. But they had plans "to bring a bit of British Columbia nature into our front yard." They spent two years planning and observing, a time they now describe as agony, before they dug in. Their goal was to create a number of different native microhabitats, from the dry to the moist, the full sun to woodland.

First, they put in the vine maples, the cedars and the waterfall, masterminding the sound so that it would reflect back into the house. They moved the large rocks that were already on the site, built retaining walls, put in flagstone paths and created a pond, using bentonite mixed with the native soil in order to get a water-impermeable layer in which they could also plant.

As enthusiastic botanists, they also explored wilderness areas, collecting seeds and cuttings (following strict ethical guidelines for collection). All the while,

The upright fertile fronds of deer fern (left) echo the perky cluster of dagger-leaved rush (middle) around the Skeltons' pond. One of the secrets of this garden's success is the mulch that Frank and Erin make from the fern fronds, fallen leaves and prunings, which they clean up in autumn and compost in a separate mix.

they were observing and learning from native-plant communities in the wild.

This knowledge was translated perfectly into the garden: a native sedum, found on rocky outcrops, here grows in a crevice in one of the retaining walls, tenaciously putting down roots in the tiniest hold. In shady areas – getting shadier every year as the vine maples grow – are more than 12 ferns native to British Columbia and groundcovers such as bunchberry, clintonia and wild ginger. Shrubs such as Labrador tea, salal, snowberry, red huckleberry and false azalea flourish, as witnessed by the prodigious self-seeding. Indeed, Frank and Erin see their role in the garden now as editors, refining the grammar of their garden's expressive language, moving things here and there.

Tying it all together is the moss – dozens of varieties. Frank describes moss as "forgiving": when they take out a plant or move something around, the moss quickly fills in, smoothing over their second thoughts with a protective spongy cover. To achieve this cover, Frank and Erin started with handfuls of sphagnum moss, which they ground in the blender, then poured over peat on the ground. Not only did the moss grow, but soon other mosses started to arrive. The success proved Frank's point: "You know you're successful when the only 'weeds' you get are volunteer natives." In other words, as happens in nature, the garden changes itself, and the gardener is left to ponder, to edit, to enjoy and to observe – frequently down on all fours, because the subtle wonder is often to be found in the small.

How appropriate that in a region of dramatic contrast, the towering trees and the tiniest mosses together compete for our attention in this successful native-plant garden.

A signature plant of the Northwest, found in the wild and in gardens, salal is a versatile and hardy evergreen shrub that can also be grown as a groundcover. It requires little care and tolerates a wide range of conditions. Salal may be common, but its virtues reward both the gardener and the birds, which feed on its prolific blue-black berries.

Woodland Wildflowers for the Northwestern Gardener

ॐ

The following plants could all be labeled, to varying degrees, invasive. And by that I mean, they are wonderfully spreading, wanton, *easy*. Given the right conditions, they'll carpet, cover and cavort. So a caveat: control!

Vanilla leaf (*Achlys triphylla*): To my mind, vanilla leaf is one of the simplest yet most beautiful woodlanders around: its smooth, green leaf is divided into three sections, and it sends up a single flower stalk covered in small, white blooms in late spring. It forms a woodland carpet (to 12 inches/30 cm). Prefers moist, well-drained soil but will do fine under the dry shade of conifers.

Wild ginger (*Asarum caudatum*): This woodland evergreen groundcover (6 inches/15 cm), with large, shiny heart-shaped leaves, carpets the forest floor. Flowers are maroon and bell-shaped in spring. Prefers humus-rich, moist soil.

Bunchberry (*Cornus canadensis*): This mat-forming, low-growing groundcover (8 inches/20 cm) is ideal in woodland gardens. Its dogwoodlike white flowers appear in spring, red to orange berries in fall. Needs well-drained, acidic soil.

Western bleeding heart (*Dicentra formosa*): This delicate but sturdy plant (to 20 inches/50 cm) has lacy leaves and hanging pink flowers in spring and summer. Full to part shade; well-drained, moist soil.

Twinflower (*Linnaea borealis*): With its shiny evergreen leaves and funnel-like whitish pink flowers in late spring through summer, this tough low-growing creeper (4 inches/10 cm) is another woodland carpeter for the garden. Sun or shade; well-drained, moist soil.

When western bleeding heart is grown as a specimen plant, its lacy foliage provides a delicate accent. Groups of plants are also an excellent groundcover. Flowers are long-lasting and have an unusual shape.

Canada mayflower (*Maianthemum canadense*): The white flower spikes of this shade-loving groundcover (16 inches/40 cm) form a stunning carpet in spring. Red berries appear in summer. Deep shade; poor to average soil.

Wood sorrel (*Oxalis oregana*): If you want a solid cover for the woodland floor, wood sorrel is it. With cloverlike leaves and small white or pinkish (with purple veins) flowers in spring, it grow to 8 inches (20 cm). Part to deep shade; rich, moist soil.

Winning Combos

- false lily of the valley, false Solomon's seal, twinflower
- deer fern, sword fern, wood sorrel
- Canada mayflower, western bleeding heart

A soothing fern corner reveals the triumphant possibilities of designing with foliage textures and shapes and shades of green in mind, rather than splashy, colorful blooms.

WOODLAND FERNS FOR THE NORTHWESTERN GARDENER

After seeing Art and Mareen Kruckeberg's Seattle, Washington, garden, I realized that for years, I've been doing a disservice to ferns by thinking of them simply as "fillers." Sure, they're great at filling in, but perhaps one of the truest tests (and greatest rewards) of a gardener's design sense is to give an area over to ferns and ferns alone. There are no splashy blasts of flower color to fall back on in such a space – just the lush richness of greens, the variety, textures and contrasts of foliage.

Maidenhair fern (*Adiantum pedatum*): The deciduous maidenhair delights with its dark wiry stems, from which thin blades fan out in a pleasing circular pattern. It grows 1 to 2 feet (30–60 cm). Full to part shade; moist soil; drought-intolerant.

Lady fern (*Athyrium filix-femina*): The bright green of this large deciduous fern (3 foot/1 m) brings light to the woodland garden, and its tapering tips at top and bottom add grace. Full to part shade; rich, moist soil.

Deer fern (*Blechnum spicant*): A signature fern for the northwestern woodland garden, deer fern is one I'd give my eastern eyeteeth for. Its narrow, leathery, pointed fronds are tidy and compact, and upright fertile fronds shoot up from the center of the clump. Evergreen, it grows 1 to 2 feet (30–60 cm). Sun to shade; moist to drier soils; drought-tolerant in shade.

Oak fern (*Gymnocarpium dryopteris*): With its bright green color and triangular shape (the triangular leaf is divided into three triangular leaflets), the deciduous oak fern is a smallish fern (up to 1 foot/30 cm) that often forms a pleasing woodland carpet, its leaves growing parallel to the ground. Full to part shade; well-drained, moist soil.

Sword fern (*Polystichum munitum*): Majestic is the word for this tall evergreen woodlander (4 foot/1.2 m). Its spiky fronds in circular clusters make it a dramatic addition to the home landscape, a bit of rainforest right outside the door. Although many people prune off old fronds in early spring to keep sword ferns looking fresh, at least one study suggests that uncropped ferns are more robust. Full to part shade; rich, dry to moist soil.

FERNS FOR DRY AREAS

- parsley fern (*Cryptogramma crispa*): sun to partial sun
- fragile fern, a.k.a. brittle fern (*Cystopteris fragilis*): sun to partial sun
- bracken (*Pteridium aquilinum*): sun to partial shade; invasive
- Oregon woodsia (*Woodsia oregana*): partial shade

Wetland Shrubs for the Northwestern Gardener

Moisture-loving shrubs such as Labrador tea (right) and western laurel (left) provide the perfect frame for a pond.

The following shrubs (except for the devil's club) are typical of bog habitat. They therefore need peat-rich, acidic, moist soil and are not demanding in terms of nutrients. (Bogs tend to be nutrient-poor environments.) You don't necessarily need to re-create a bog, but you do need acidic, peaty, moist soil.

The exotic-looking devil's club, by the way, is found in the wild in moist woods – in coastal forests and, in the Interior, in cedar-hemlock ecosystems.

Bog rosemary (*Andromeda polifolia*): With its rolled leathery leaf edges and small, pink urnlike flowers, this low-growing evergreen shrub (20–32 inches/50–80 cm) is a good addition to a rock garden. Leaves turn purplish bronze in winter. Sun to part shade; moist, acidic, peat-rich soil.

Western laurel, a.k.a. alpine laurel (*Kalmia microphylla* var.*occidentalis*): Very close to the bog rosemary in appearance, this small evergreen shrub grows to 20 inches (50 cm) and produces pink saucerlike flowers in late spring and early summer. Sun to part shade.

Labrador tea (*Ledum groenlandicum*): This fragrant evergreen shrub thrives in poor soil. Growing to approximately 5 feet (1.5 m), it has narrow leaves that look almost leathery and turn under at the margin. Its white pompomlike flower clusters attract bees and are a delight in early summer. Sun to part shade; moist, acidic, poor soil.

Sweet gale (*Myrica gale*): A low-growing, fragrant, erect deciduous shrub (5 feet/1.5 m), sweet gale grows naturally in bogs. Greenish flowers are borne on catkins. Sun to part shade; acidic soil.

Devil's club (*Oplopanax horridus*): More magical than diabolical (though it does have painful spines), devil's club is a striking deciduous shrub. It grows tall (3–10 feet/1–3 m) with large maplelike leaves and white flowers on a pyramidal cluster in late spring/early summer. The shiny red berries ripen in late summer. Full shade to filtered sun.

Hardhack (*Spiraea douglasii*): Growing naturally around ponds, in wet meadows and in bogs, hardhack is spectacular in early summer when topped with showy pink plumes. It is fast-growing (invasive even), reaching 6 to 7 feet (2 m). Its winter twig form is also attractive, topped with brownish husks. Full sun to part shade; rich soil.

Bog cranberry (*Vaccinium oxycoccos*, a.k.a. *Oxycoccus oxycoccos*): This creeping evergreen shrub produces pinkish red flowers and berries that turn from white to red as they ripen. Sun; acidic, peat-rich boggy conditions.

A Wetland Wonder

Port Orchard, Washington

It's an unusual gardener who says with glee, "Here, let me show you my swamp." But in his Port Orchard, Washington, wetland garden, Bob Wiltermood is doing wonderful work to recuperate the word, revealing the beauty, complexity and biological richness of that much-maligned aquatic system.

To the wary, the word *swamp* often conjures images of dank, mucky places; in Bob's swamp, one is more likely to find bright humor, such as the little rubber duck or two upended rubber boots sticking out of the water, sly remnants of a party gone wild.

In our fevered rush to develop "waste places," we've drained, filled, paved, "improved" and otherwise destroyed many a wetland swamp in North America. But Bob's swamp shows that such places are alive with animals and plants. He tells stories of the otter running across the lawn with a goldfish in its mouth ("it's just the way it is; can't get worried about it"), the mountain beaver living near the deck, the mink and the 58 species of nesting birds that make their home here. When I ask where the mosquitoes are, Bob tells me that he gets bitten by mosquitoes only when he goes to the city.

The secret of wetlands, says Bob Wiltermood, is lots of LOD: Large Organic Debris. Logs laid horizontally provide platforms for the birds to march along in their hopping tromp to the water. Stumps and snags, such as the old fir tree here, are used by pileated woodpeckers. Fish lurk under submerged dead trees, and on the shore, huge tangles of old brush provide habitat piles for wildlife.

Bob Wiltermood's wetland garden manages to combine two competing impulses and still come up with a coherent whole. The plantings are wild, even chaotic in their lush randomness, yet the human design elements, such as the deck, which seems to float above the wetland, point to control and symmetry. (As Bob puts it, "I like my straight lines.") The result: The wild and the tame coexist beautifully in the garden.

The University of British Columbia Native Plant Garden is well worth a visit for northwestern gardeners on a hunt for design inspiration and plant-combination ideas. In the pond garden, skunk cabbages emerge from the watery depths.

Wetland Wildflowers for the Northwestern Gardener

From full-scale pond to seasonally wet spots, water gardening offers a wide palette of plants from which to choose. And there's something so satisfying about digging in rich, mucky soil – I suspect it harks back to childhood admonitions. As adults, we're finally allowed the thrill of wallowing in a soggy mess of soaking soil.

Marsh marigold (*Caltha biflora*): A short charmer (4–16 inches/10–40 cm), marsh marigold has bright shiny leaves and white flowers with yellow centers. Also try yellow marsh marigold (*Caltha palustris* subsp. *asarifolia*) for its yellow flowers. Full sun to part shade; thrives in shallow parts of ponds (4–6 inches/10–15 cm) as well.

Skunk cabbage, a.k.a. swamp lantern (*Lysichiton americanum*): The common skunk cabbage is unfortunately, though appropriately, named (it does have a faint skunky smell when in flower). Its yellow flowers, protected by a bright yellow hood, appear early in spring, then its huge leaves take over. It grows 1 to 3 feet (30–90 cm). Full sun to shade; moist soil.

Bogbean, a.k.a. buckbean (*Menyanthes trifoliata*): Another stinker, bogbean thrives in the water. Its trifoliate leaves look almost beseeching, and its frilly whitish pink flowers appear in spring. Plant in pots in a pond. Sun.

Yellow pond-lily, a.k.a. yellow waterlily (*Nuphar polysepalum*, a.k.a. *N. luteum* subsp. *polysepalum*): In a pond, you can't beat the drama of this one. Huge, heart-shaped leaves float on the surface, and yellow flowers bloom through the summer. Requires a deep pond. Full sun; calm water.

Green false hellebore (*Veratrum viride*): With its large leaves, tall, tasseled flower clusters and great height (3–6 feet/1–2 m), this plant is dramatic – and poisonous too. Sun to part shade.

The perky leaves of bogbean look almost beseeching as they shoot up from the pond at the University of British Columbia Native Plant Garden.

GARDENING TO PROTECT STREAMS

A watercourse at Bloedel Reserve on Bainbridge Island, Washington, meanders through a cushiony bed of moss and wood sorrel.

If you have a natural stream running through your property, you also have a wonderful opportunity to have a positive impact on the water quality of the whole stream. The vegetation that grows along the banks of a stream or river – called riparian vegetation – serves extremely important functions: preventing erosion; trapping sediment and pollution; dissipating floodwaters; providing a home for wildlife species. Thus, by protecting and enhancing the riparian vegetation, you're also protecting and enhancing the life of the stream.

Grasses, Rushes and Sedges: slough grass (*Beckmannia syzigachne*); slough sedge (*Carex obnupta*); creeping spike rush (*Eleocharis palustris*); western manna grass (*Glyceria occidentalis*); and dagger-leaved rush (*Juncus ensifolius*). All prefer sun and plenty of moisture.

Shrubs (moisture-loving shrubs help to stabilize the soil and provide important wildlife habitat): serviceberry (*Amelanchier alnifolia*); red-osier dogwood (*Cornus sericea*); black twinberry (*Lonicera involucrata*); ninebark (*Physocarpus capitatus*); cluster rose (*Rosa pisocarpa*); thimbleberry (*Rubus parviflorus*); salmonberry (*Rubus spectabilis*); and blue elderberry (*Sambucus caerulea*).

Trees: vine maple (*Acer circinatum*); Oregon ash (*Fraxinus latifolia*); black cottonwood (*Populus trichocarpa*); and Pacific willow (*Salix lucida* subsp. *lasiandra*).

As the King County Surface Water Management agency in Washington State reminds us: "Everyone lives downstream."

Source: *Stream and Wetland Enhancement Guide* by Mark G. Wilson, Dennis O'Connor and USA staff, published by Unified Sewerage Agency, Hillsboro, Oregon.

The large reddish flowers of salmonberry are a knockout in spring, and the plant's yellowy orange to red berries are tasty. Salmonberry is a good shrub for the wilder sections of the garden, as it often forms dense tangles.

Splendor of the Grass
and a Beguiling Bog

Portland, Oregon

Nestled under a deck, Mike McKeag's bog mimics the feel of a bog found beneath a deeply shaded forest canopy. Draped shade cloth provides further light protection until the natural shading of elderberry and thimbleberry is established. An added bonus: The upper deck feels as if it is floating on a sea of elderberry. In the foreground is a large clump of skunk cabbage.

MIKE MCKEAG CONFESSES that he spent the summer of 1993 on his knees – weeding, that is. It wasn't the field of Queen Anne's lace, Canada thistle and Johnson grass that did it. He'd already collected thirty 30-gallon (115 L) bags of *that* problem in 1991. Instead, it was the weed seeds lurking in the soil that led to his summer battle of hand-to-hand combat.

Gardening, I'm convinced, is all about time and change and about negotiating a working relationship between human pace and nature's pace. Tell that to the weeds, Mike might say – and he's earned his grumpiness stripes, although surprisingly, he never seems to wear them. To lose two years of good growing time in a project of such grand scale would be a severe blow to most gardeners, but Mike talks about that time in terms of opportunity and the chance to learn.

Mike McKeag and Kathleen McAllister's odyssey began in the summer of 1991. Mike originally wanted to live on a houseboat but, instead, took on a landscape project that was the opposite of carefree landlessness: on a 60-by-110-foot (18 m x 33 m) lot in Portland, Oregon, he decided to create a number of different habitats – pond, stream, bog, hedgerow, thicket and meadow bisected by the stream – using plants native to the Willamette Valley and neighboring hills of Oregon.

First came the bulldozer to do the grading around the house, sculpt a berm and create a hollow for the pond. Then came a water-garden contractor to dig a stream course that meanders down to the pond.

The meadow called for the highest level of scrutiny. The native bunchgrass (red fescue), seeded early on after the weeds were eliminated, created a monoculture – the opposite of a healthy and diverse meadow community full of different native grasses and wildflowers. If he had it to do all over again, Mike would plant plugs of various native grasses, building diversity into the system right from the start.

"I need only slide open my patio door and take six steps, and I am sitting beside a rushing stream, watching the sun set behind distant firs, as swallows skim the pond and wind rustles willow leaves and works the flowering tops of meadow grasses," says Mike McKeag. The stream was created by digging a trench, then edging the sides with stones discreetly mortared in place. The rubber liner of the stream and pond was coated with a thick, protective layer of mortar, onto which river cobbles were scattered to make the stream bottom look more natural.

Red-flowering currant is guaranteed to attract hummingbirds to the garden.

As a visual barrier between the house and the street, Mike's berm, a relatively dry, exposed site, consists of a thicket of vine maple, tall Oregon grape, serviceberry, ocean-spray, mock orange and red-flowering currant. Native red fescue covers the ground of the berm, with June grass on the crest.

His bog was an immediate triumph. As Mike points out, "Most homeowners consider a wet spot in the yard a problem. But we went to considerable trouble and some expense to create one. It's not a problem; it's an opportunity, and it can be a source of great pleasure." Sheltered by a deck whose wooden slats mimic the dappled light under a forest canopy, the bog garden provides pleasure to the senses, from its deep musty scent to its cool glowing greens. It feels like a hidden, protected place, perfect for escape.

The oxalis and skunk cabbage, suggested by a visit to a local bog, have now filled in with new lady ferns, thimbleberry, devil's club, false Solomon's seal and wild ginger. The elderberry and thimbleberry shrubs, planted around the perimeter, provide protective cover, not only for the bog but also for the robin, sitting on her second brood when I visited in June.

Indeed, the birds reveal the fundamental principle at work in Mike's garden: "We aren't interested in creating a static ornament. We are playing with processes, reveling in the knowledge that we are not the only agents at work here." The other agents include birds, the mysterious creature that visits the pond some nights and digs up the juncus, and the wild strawberry, which made up Mike's mind for him while he tried to decide what groundcover to use. These "agents" obligingly offer up beauty and, just as important, stridently announce the need for refinements.

But Mike doesn't resent such lessons: yes, he has to live with the consequences of red fescue turned monoculture, for example, but the Indian plum in full bloom connects him intimately, exuberantly, aesthetically and emotionally with all the Indian plums blooming in wild places throughout the region: "The communion is the same as if I'd driven 200 miles and pitched my tent."

Sun-Loving Shrubs for the Northwestern Gardener

In drought-prone areas of the Northwest, acres and acres of thirsty lawns seem even more of a monocultural monstrosity than they do elsewhere. How much more appropriate, when looking for a low-maintenance groundcover, to choose a native low-growing shrub, such as kinnikinnick or creeping juniper.

Serviceberry, a.k.a. saskatoon (*Amelanchier alnifolia*): A delightful large shrub (16–17 feet/5 m), serviceberry has attractive and fragrant white flowers in spring, dark blue fruit that is loved by wildlife in summer and yellow leaves in autumn. Sun to part shade; moist to dry sites; tolerates poor soil.

Kinnikinnick (*Arctostaphylos uva-ursi*): This trailing evergreen shrub is a perfect low groundcover (4–8 inches/10–20 cm) in poor soil. The drooping flowers are pinkish white and appear in spring. Bright red berries last throughout the fall – if the birds leave any, that is. Perfect for soil stabilization on slopes or as a drought-tolerant lawn alternative. Sun; dry, poor soil.

Ocean-spray (*Holodiscus discolor*): When this deciduous shrub is in flower, it's obvious why it is so named – foamy conical clusters of creamy white flowers cover the plant in midsummer. Growing 5 to 16 feet (1.5–5 m), ocean-spray prefers open conditions. Full sun to open shade; well-drained soil; drought-tolerant.

Creeping juniper (*Juniperus horizontalis*): A low-maintenance groundcover, creeping juniper creates a carpet of bluish green (evergreen, in fact). It grows to 1 foot (30 cm). Sun; good drainage.

Mock orange (*Philadelphus lewisii*): With its profusion of fragrant white blossoms in late spring/early summer, this deciduous shrub is highly ornamental and a good nectar source for butterflies. It grows to 10 feet (3 m) in a variety of conditions. Sun to part shade; dry to moist soil; drought-tolerant.

Shrubby cinquefoil (*Potentilla fruticosa*): This deciduous deerproof shrub grows to about 3 feet (1 m) high, with velvety leaves and bright yellow flowers throughout the summer. Full sun; good drainage.

Red-flowering currant (*Ribes sanguineum*): This plant is a knockout when rose-pink flowers are in bloom and the branches arch under their weight in early spring. (Mike McKeag offers the most sanguine description: "The whole bush bursts in a spectacular hemorrhage.") It grows quickly, up to 10 feet (3 m). Flowers attract hummingbirds; blue-black berries attract birds. Red-flowering currant does well in moist open woods, but don't plant it with white pine, as red-flowering currant is a host plant for white pine blister rust. Sun to part shade; well-drained mesic to dry soil.

Nootka rose (*Rosa nutkana*): For both its flowers (large and pink, appearing in early summer) and its hips (large and purplish red), this deciduous native rose deserves a place in the garden. It grows to 10 feet (3 m). Full sun; rich soil; drought-tolerant.

Snowberry (*Symphoricarpos albus*): With tiny purplish white bell-shaped flowers in spring, snowberry is a low-growing, erect deciduous shrub (6–7 feet/2 m). Clusters of white berries appear in late summer and last through winter, attracting birds. Although susceptible to powdery mildew, snowberry forms thickets and thus is good for soil-stabilization projects on steep banks. Part shade to sun; dry to moist soil.

Ocean-spray is spectacular in midsummer when it is covered with creamy white blooms, but this shrub also looks great with its reddish leaves in autumn and its dried flower clusters in winter.

In a primarily nonnative plant corner, columbine provides a bright native accent.

Sun-Loving Wildflowers for the Northwestern Gardener

Perhaps it is a question that should be directed to sociologists rather than gardeners, but I often wonder why so many of our beautiful native plants are relatively underused in the cultivated landscape. The following natives offer just as much color and interesting form as the more popular exotic plants, so why not invite these beauties through the garden gate?

Pearly everlasting (*Anaphalis margaritacea*): Blooming in midsummer and growing from 1 to 3 feet (30–90 cm), pearly everlasting is considered by some to be almost weedy because it is so robust and spreading, but its beautiful clusters of white flowers and silvery foliage make it a graceful garden plant. Sun to partial sun; poor soil with good drainage; drought-tolerant.

Columbine (*Aquilegia formosa*): A versatile, easy-to-grow, readily self-seeding plant, columbine has reddish orange and yellow flowers that nod on thin stems in early summer. It grows 1 to 3 feet (30–90 cm) and attracts hummingbirds and butterflies. Full sun to part shade; average garden soil.

Sea pink, a.k.a. thrift (*Armeria maritima*): On poor, shallow soil in meadows and bluffs, sea pink thrives. Its pink flower heads are round and small, its leaves grasslike. It grows to about 8 inches (20 cm) and blooms throughout the summer. Full sun.

Common harebell, a.k.a. bluebell of Scotland (*Campanula rotundifolia*): Delicate bell-shaped purplish blue flowers bloom in summer. Leaves are round at the base of the plant and narrow higher up. Grows 6 to 18 inches (15–45 cm). Average to moist soil; sun.

Oregon sunshine, a.k.a. woolly sunflower (*Eriophyllum lanatum*): This cheerful yellow daisylike flower delights in early summer. Shear it after first bloom, and it will flower again in early fall. The leaves are narrow, bluish and woolly. It grows to 2 feet (60 cm). Sun; dry soil.

Tiger lily, a.k.a. Columbia lily, Oregon lily (*Lilium columbianum*): Very showy nodding orange blooms dotted with dark purplish brown appear throughout the summer. It grows 1 to 3 feet (30–90 cm). Purchase only from nurseries which guarantee that plants are not dug from the wild. Sun; moist soil.

Lomatium, a.k.a. barestem desert-parsley, pestle parsnip (*Lomatium nudicaule*): I'm a sucker for glaucous leaves, and lomatium delivers them. Not only that, but its flowers are attractive (small and yellow) and its seeds delicious (intense celery flavor), and it is a butterfly-larva host plant. It grows 1 to 3 feet (30–90 cm). Sun; dry soil.

Large-leaved lupine (*Lupinus polyphyllus*): Everything about this plant demands admiration: its palmate leaves, its showy blue flowers and its soil-enriching capabilities (a legume, it fixes nitrogen in the soil). It grows to about 4 feet (1.2 m). If crowded, it is susceptible to powdery mildew, which may decrease the plant's vigor but won't kill it. Full sun; moist soil.

Penstemon (*Penstemon cardwellii*): With its masses of rosy purple flowers in early summer, this sprawling plant creates a gorgeous, colorful carpet. The flowers attract hummingbirds. It grows to 1 foot (30 cm). Full sun; well-drained soil.

Graceful cinquefoil (*Potentilla gracilis*): Small, yellow flowers are borne on top of slender, branching stems – hence the grace. Grows to 2 feet (60 cm) and blooms in summer. Average to dry soil; sun. The related Pacific silverweed (*P. anserina* subsp. *pacifica*) is a low-growing groundcover (10 inches/25 cm) with silky, silvery leaves and yellow flowers in summer; suitable for moist areas in sun.

Broad-leaved stonecrop (*Sedum spathulifolium*): Succulent leaves (some glaucous, some reddish), masses of long-lasting, starlike yellow flowers in late spring and early summer, drought tolerance – what more could you ask for in a groundcover? Perfect for the rock garden, it grows to about 8 inches (20 cm). Full sun; well-drained soil; drought-tolerant.

This front-yard meadow garden is drought-tolerant and low maintenance, two unbeatable benefits of gardening with native plants. The yellow potentilla and reddish orange columbine are two of the easiest sun-loving perennials to grow in the Northwest.

For erosion control on steep, sunny slopes, native-plant expert Clay Antieau suggests goldenrod (*Solidago canadensis*), pearly everlasting (*Anaphalis margaritacea*) and Douglas' aster (*Aster subspicatus*).

TIPS ON MEADOW-MAKING

- Remove all existing nonnative grasses; you need to start with a clean soil bed.
- Use plugs rather than seeds of native grasses so that you can more easily control the variety and distribution of grass species.
- Meadow Grasses: California oat-grass (*Danthonia californica*); Idaho fescue (*Festuca idahoensis*); western fescue (*Festuca occidentalis*); red fescue (*Festuca rubra*); crested June grass (*Koeleria cristata*).

It seems ironic that Interstate 84 delivers travelers to some of the most gorgeous scenery in all of Oregon – the Columbia River Gorge – yet the highway itself cuts a depressing strip. But at Milepost 68, something different awaits. This is the site of Chicken Charley Flat, a native-plant restoration project started in 1989 by Russ Jolley, the Native Plant Society of Oregon and the Portland Garden Club in cooperation with the Oregon Department of Transportation.

Originally a desolate patch covered with nonnative weeds, its heavily compacted soil mainly rocks, Chicken Charley Flat is now a budding pine-oak savanna. Using native seed found within a one-mile (1.6 km) radius of the site, volunteers planted the 1,000-foot-long (305 m) strip with 35 species of wildflowers, five species of bunchgrasses and a variety of native shrubs. Seventeen native species have since shown up on their own.

Close to Chicken Charlie Flat on I-84 is another meadow-landscaping project at the Mosier Interchange at Exit 69, also involving volunteers from the Native Plant Society of Oregon and spearheaded by Jerry and Mike Igo. Here, Oregon sunshine is taking hold, brightening the highway strip with native beauty.

Drought-Tolerant Natives for the Northwestern Gardener

In the good old days, before the greenhouse effect and ozone-layer depletion were a part of every school kid's vocabulary, we were equally blind to the effects of our profligate water use. Now, there's no excuse for denial.

Summer droughts are a fact of northwestern life, and many native plants have evolved adaptive mechanisms to cope with drought: the waxy coating on the needles of native conifers, for example, helps to limit water loss from the trees; and the curling leaves and fuzzy undersides of some shrubs, such as Labrador tea, help to conserve moisture. And many of these drought-tolerant natives are showy and easy to grow.

Trees: Douglas maple (*Acer glabrum*); rocky mountain juniper (*Juniperus scopulorum*); shore pine (*Pinus contorta*).

Shrubs: serviceberry (*Amelanchier alnifolia*); hairy manzanita (*Arctostaphylos columbiana*); deerbrush (*Ceanothus integerrimus*); ocean-spray (*Holodiscus discolor*); common juniper (*Juniperus communis*); dull Oregon grape (*Mahonia nervosa*); Indian plum (*Oemleria cerasiformis*); mock orange (*Philadelphus lewisii*); red-flowering currant (*Ribes sanguineum*); buffaloberry (*Shepherdia canadensis*); snowberry (*Symphoricarpos albus*).

Wildflowers: nodding onion (*Allium cernuum*); pearly everlasting (*Anaphalis margaritacea*); sea pink (*Armeria maritima*); Oregon sunshine (*Eriophyllum lanatum*); small-flowered alum root (*Heuchera micrantha*); lewisia (*Lewisia cotyledon*); lowbush penstemon (*Penstemon fruticosus*); shrubby cinquefoil (*Potentilla fruticosa*); broad-leaved stonecrop (*Sedum spathulifolium*).

Drought-tolerant small-flowered alum root creates an airy display. The bluish leaves behind are lomatium; the small, white flowers (lower right) are fool's onion.

Groundcovers and Vines: vanilla leaf (*Achlys triphylla*); kinnikinnick (*Arctostaphylos uva-ursi*); rock clematis (*Clematis columbiana*); coastal strawberry (*Fragaria chiloensis*); wild strawberry (*Fragaria virginiana*); western trumpet honeysuckle (*Lonicera ciliosa*).

Ferns: spiny wood fern (*Dryopteris expansa*); sword fern (*Polystichum munitum*). Deer fern (*Blechnum spicant*) is drought-tolerant in shade.

Sources: Corinne Kennedy, "Drought-Tolerant Native Plants," *Douglasia*, volume 19, number 4 (Fall 1995), pp. 16–18, and *Naturescape Native Plant and Animal Booklet, Georgia Basin* by Susan Campbell (Victoria: Naturescape, 1995). See also *Sagebrush Country: A Wildflower Sanctuary* by Ronald J. Taylor (Missoula: Mountain Press Publishing, 1992).

Northwestern Rock-Garden Plants

What exactly makes a plant suitable for a rock garden?
I guess it all depends on how one defines a rock garden.
The classic rock garden is a miniature composition of
subtle grace, composed primarily of low-growing plants
and artfully arranged rocks in a sunny site, often on slop-
ing or uneven terrain. And there are oodles of northwestern natives to fit this habitat bill, thanks to the West's
mountainous regions.

The northwestern rock gardener has a huge plant
palette from which to choose – from the subalpine parkland of mountain meadows and rocky outcrops to the
alpine tundra of the tree line, from the Cascade Mountains east to the Rockies. As well, many of the grassland
species typical of low-lying interior habitats will also be
at home in the rock garden.

Wildflowers and Ferns: Hooker's onion (*Allium acuminatum*); balsamroot (*Balsamorhiza sagittata*); common
harebell (*Campanula rotundifolia*); lace fern (*Cheilanthes
gracillima*); parsley fern (*Cryptogramma crispa*); few-
flowered shooting star (*Dodecatheon pulchellum*); fleabane (*Erigeron compositus*); iris (*Iris innominata*);
Oregon iris (*Iris tenax*); lewisia (*Lewisia cotyledon*); penstemon (*Penstemon davidsonii*); phlox (*Phlox diffusa*);
cinquefoil (*Potentilla breweri*); broad-leaved stonecrop
(*Sedum spathulifolium*); moss campion (*Silene acaulis*).
Shrubs and Groundcovers: kinnikinnick (*Arctostaphylos
uva ursi*); mahala mat (*Ceanothus prostratus*);
common juniper (*Juniperus communis*); dwarf willow
(*Salix arctica*).

For more information on native rock-garden plants
for the Northwest, see *Rocky Mountain Alpines* edited by J.
Williams (Portland: Timber Press, 1986) and *Mountain
Plants of the Pacific Northwest* by Ronald J. Taylor
and George W. Douglas (Missoula: Mountain Press
Publishing, 1995).

Thanks to a slew of volunteers, a local neighborhood coalition
and the City of Portland Parks Bureau, Macadam Bay Butterfly
Park – once a construction dump, then a parking lot – is now a
half-acre (0.2 ha) shortgrass prairie, a haven of butterfly habitat
in the midst of the city.

The garden was covered in the soft down of cottonwoods
the day I visited, giving an altogether fleeting and feathery
feeling to the place. Here, the blue penstemon rises above the
yellow graceful cinquefoil.

Native grasses used in the garden include blue wild rye,
California brome, Idaho fescue and red fescue. Native perennials
include alum root, blue field gilia, cliff larkspur, columbine,
goldenrod, graceful cinquefoil, lomatium, Oregon sunshine,
pearly everlasting and riverbank lupine.

Western Weeds to Watch Out For

♨

In a kind of botanical magical mystery tour in the early 1990s, members of the Washington Native Plant Society retraced the steps of 19th-century botanical explorer Louis F. Henderson in order to collect specimens and answer the question: How has the region's flora changed in the past hundred years? In a project spearheaded by Sarah Gage and Sharon Rodman, the modern-day explorers reported in *Douglasia* that unfortunately, "invasive alien weeds are [now] everywhere. In some places, that's all there is."

And if not all, then a high proportion. Gerald Straley and Patrick Harrison conducted a botanical inventory of the University of British Columbia's Endowment Lands, and by 1987, they had identified 384 species, 220 (or 57 percent) of which were nonnatives. "Garden escapees are constantly being brought in accidentally or intentionally or dumped with garden refuse," they report in *An Illustrated Flora of the University Endowment Lands*. "Some of these persist for a few years, and many others become permanent residents."

"Invasive" does indeed capture the marauding spirit of too much of the nonnative vegetation that has tenaciously set down roots in the Northwest. Scotch broom, for example, while beautiful, turns once diverse meadows into biologically monotonous monocultures. Himalaya blackberry transforms rich thickets into tangled masses of one species. Herb robert crowds out native understory species in woodlands. English ivy kills trees and suppresses understory vegetation. Purple loosestrife turns productive wetlands into single stands of purple menace. And on and on goes the list of species that are crowding out natives and outcompeting indigenous vegetation in native habitats.

The following is a list of some invasive species which are spreading in the wild in the Northwest and which gardeners should be especially careful to keep out of their landscapes. Pull on first sighting before these plants gain a toehold and spread to wild areas.

(For more information on invasive exotics, contact municipal, county, state or provincial officials for a copy of the noxious-weed list for your region, or get in touch with the Washington Native Plant Society.)

Invasive Species: European beachgrass (*Ammophila arenaria*); wormwood (*Artemisia absinthium*); knapweed (*Centaurea maculosa*); Scotch broom (*Cytisus scoparius*); spurge laurel (*Daphne laureola*); great globe thistle (*Echinops sphaerocephalus*); herb robert (*Geranium robertianum*); baby's breath (*Gypsophila paniculata*); English ivy (*Hedera helix*); giant hogweed (*Heracleum mantegazzianum*); *Hydrilla verticillata*; yellow water iris (*Iris pseudacorus*); Dalmatian toadflax (*Linaria genistifolia* var. *dalmatica*); purple loosestrife (*Lythrum salicaria*); four o'clock (*Mirabilis nyctaginea*); reed canary grass (*Phalaris arundinacea*) – native, but since European settlement, it has become invasive; unicorn plant (*Proboscidea louisianica*); cherry laurel (*Prunus laurocerasus*); Himalaya blackberry (*Rubus discolor*, a.k.a. *R. procerus*); tamarisk (*Tamarix chinensis*); gorse (*Ulex europaeus*).

Two excellent publications to help identify weeds in the Northwest are: *Northwest Weeds: The Ugly and Beautiful Villains of Fields, Gardens and Roadsides* by Ronald J. Taylor (Missoula, Montana: Mountain Press, 1990) and *Weeds of the West*, edited by T.D. Whitson (Western Society of Weed Science, 1990), available from WSU Cooperative Extension, P.O. Box 645912, Washington State University, Pullman, Washington 99164–5912.

Garry Oak Meadows

Richard Hebda, a native-plant expert, writes, "The Garry oak's tolerance of a wide variety of conditions, especially drought, and its remarkable resilience to damage and disturbance make it ideally suited to ornamental uses in the urban and suburban landscape."

The Garry Oak Meadow Preservation Society can be reached at 3873 Swan Lake Road, Victoria, British Columbia V8X 3W1.

I'm a longtime oak fan, but I wasn't prepared to fall in love with the West Coast's Garry oaks. I feel personally wounded when people call these trees "messy" or "ugly." More appropriate terms, to my mind, unfortunately form a litany of clichés: majestic, enchanting, haunting, magical.

Whatever, Garry oaks are simply splendid trees. In winter, their gnarled, twisty branches form an arresting silhouette against the sky. Their trunks and branches, delicately encrusted with lichens and a spongy layer of bryophytes, delight with subtle shifts of color and texture. In summer, their thick, shiny leaves – sometimes curled – create a dazzling shimmer and a slight clacking in the wind: the upper side of each leaf is a glossy green, while the underside is a paler green. With each rustle, a sparkling shift of hue conducts an entrancing dance.

But my love for the Garry oaks in Victoria, British Columbia, began to take the depressing form of unrequited longing: Where were the Garry oak seedlings, I wondered, the next generation of trees to replace the aging? Why were so many specimens reduced to botanical isolation, surrounded by clipped lawns? Where were the oaks' associated meadow species – the camas lilies, and so on?

If someone were to ask what ecosystem is most threatened on the West Coast, I suspect that most of us would say the temperate rainforest. While there's little doubt that the temperate rainforest is indeed under threat – and efforts to preserve it deserve our support – the Garry oak meadow community is, in fact, one of the most threatened landscapes in British Columbia (indeed, in Canada) and is also, for a number of reasons, suffering from ecological degradation in Washington and Oregon.

Happily, work is being done to protect and restore the Garry oak meadow community. Much credit for this has to go to the Garry Oak Meadow Preservation Society, a volunteer group based in Victoria, British Columbia. Dozens of other local groups have also swung into high gear, including the West Coast Ecological Youth Alliance, the Mount Tolmie Conservancy Association in Victoria and even the Girl Guides.

THERE ARE TREMENDOUS opportunities for gardeners to help reverse the loss of Garry oak habitat and, at the same time, create gorgeous meadows in their own yards.

The most visually dramatic rewards come in spring, before the oaks leaf out, when the understory meadow is ablaze with color. The symphony starts in February and early March with blue-eyed Mary, yellow monkey-flower, pinkish purple shooting star, spring gold and purple satin flower. As March turns to April, blue camas lily, white fawn lily and pink sea blush appear, along with white miner's lettuce and yellow western buttercup. Into May, the blues of larkspur move in, punctuated by the white of small-flowered alum root and the purplish brown of the chocolate lily. By summer, blue harvest brodiaea, pink Hooker's onion and yellow broad-leaved stonecrop form the floral backdrop against the increasingly long grass carpet.

All these Garry oak denizens are perfect for cultivation in the garden. The key is to attend to the plants' needs, and that requires a radical rethinking of conventional maintenance techniques. Most important: no mowing until July, after these spring-blooming natives have completed their flowering cycle and set seed. And no watering: the Garry oak meadow species are adapted to drought conditions. In other words, you'll need to get used to the long-dry-grass look.

Hans Roemer, who for close to a decade has been trying to enhance a Garry oak meadow on his Victoria, British Columbia, property, reports that his main task as a gardener is to help plants flourish in a near-natural site. To do this, he tries to ensure that maximum sunlight reaches the meadow plants and that they're subject to minimal competition. For example, he mows in July and then again in late December or in January, which gets rid of any regrowth, especially after a wet fall or mild winter. Hans believes that the July mowing not only helps the natives scatter their seeds but also keeps nonnative perennial grasses in check. The main problem now, he finds, is cat's ear, a nonnative weed that demands constant vigilance. His original main problem, however, was Scotch broom, and to hear that he spent four years of intensive pulling and cutting before production dropped off is indeed discouraging. But after seven years, he reports that finally, there are no new broom seedlings.

In Canada, Garry oaks occur mainly on the southeast coast of Vancouver Island, on the Gulf Islands and in a few small isolated sites on the mainland. In the United States, Garry oak meadow habitat forms a thin inland strip stretching from Puget Sound in Washington to California, with a small eastward jog along the Pit River and Columbia Gorge in Oregon.

A Meadow Symphony

Victoria, British Columbia

The rich color of camas lily can create a sea of blue in the spring garden.

I KNEW WE WERE getting close to Don Vincent's (1926–1997) garden because of the traffic jam. It's not that he lived on a major street; it's that his Victoria garden is a major showstopper in spring. The cars lined the residential street as people hopped out to take photographs and marvel at the exuberant display.

Victoria is well known for exuberant displays. In a province of gardeners, the city is world-renowned for its floral beauty and the care with which residents cultivate their gardens. But Victoria is rapidly becoming known for another floral triumph: the beauty of its native – and now sadly endangered – plant community, the Garry oak meadow.

With more than 20 mature Garry oaks dotting the half-acre (0.2 ha) property, it's the understory meadow, with its riotous spring color, that causes cars to stop in front of Don's garden. Imagine a sea of bright blue, a carpet of camas lilies – literally hundreds – covering the ground, practically sparkling in the spring light. Closer inspection reveals variety too – the chocolate lilies (when the Vincents moved in more than 20 years ago, there were just a few; now dozens bloom) and white fawn lilies scattered throughout, deep purples and whites punctuating the mass of blue.

I assumed that such a spectacular display took years of work, but Don set me straight: "People ask me, how did you do that? And I say, do nothing! The camas lilies have been there for 10,000 years. If there's a dormant seedbed of camas in your lawn or a seed source close by so that seeds will be deposited, just sit back, and don't cut the grass." Benign neglect was never sweeter.

Don Vincent's Garry oak meadow garden in Victoria, British Columbia, is a showstopper in spring when the camas lilies are in bloom.

In Victoria, British Columbia, Beacon Hill Park is one of the best places to enjoy camas lilies in bloom, seen here with western buttercup.

NATIVE GRASSES AND SHRUBS FOR GARRY OAK MEADOWS

Though many gardeners have had success growing Garry oak meadow species such as camas lilies in nonnative lawn grasses, why not experiment with native grasses, some of which are available as seed in the nursery trade. As well, the following shrubs are all readily available from garden centers.

Grasses: California brome (*Bromus carinatus*); blue wild rye (*Elymus glaucus*); Idaho fescue (*Festuca idahoensis*); western fescue (*Festuca occidentalis*); Alaska oniongrass (*Melica subulata*).

Shrubs: serviceberry (*Amelanchier alnifolia*); ocean-spray (*Holodiscus discolor*); tall Oregon grape (*Mahonia aquifolium*); Indian plum (*Oemleria cerasiformis*); mock orange (*Philadelphus lewisii*); red-flowering currant (*Ribes sanguineum*); Nootka rose (*Rosa nutkana*); snowberry (*Symphoricarpos albus*).

GARRY OAK MEADOW PLANTS FOR THE NORTHWEST

Hooker's onion, a.k.a. ornamental onion, pink wild onion (*Allium acuminatum*): An early-summer bloomer, the leaves wither prior to the appearance of the pinkish purple urn-shaped flowers. It grows to approximately 1 foot (30 cm).

Harvest brodiaea, a.k.a. harvest lily (*Brodiaea coronaria*): These violet-purple flowers, which appear in early summer, are funnel-shaped and set atop a leafless stalk (the leaves dry out before the flowers bloom) that grows to approximately 1 foot (30 cm).

Common camas (*Camassia quamash*): This is the signature plant of the Garry oak meadow – and the source of early pioneers' descriptions of stunning "seas of blue." Blooming in spring, this bulb sends up a 1-to-2-foot (30–60 cm) stem with a gorgeous blue flower. Also

WINNING COMBOS

- broad-leaved shooting star, common camas, white fawn lily
- common camas, death camas
- broad-leaved shooting star, broad-leaved stonecrop, sea blush
- common camas, western buttercup
- broad-leaved shooting star, chocolate lily, white fawn lily
- ocean-spray, white fawn lily
- broad-leaved stonecrop, kinnikinnick

try great camas (*C. leichtlinii*), which grows west of the Cascade Mountains, from southern British Columbia to California. Both have naturally occurring white forms that are available commercially.

Broad-leaved shooting star (*Dodecatheon hendersonii*): Appropriately named, these stunning pink flowers, with yellow and magenta highlights, look as if they are marauding a path through the sky. (In more prosaic moments, they also remind me of badminton birdies, but who would name a flower after that?) Leaves are broad and low to the ground, and the flower stalk grows to about 1 foot (30 cm).

White fawn lily, a.k.a. Oregon fawn lily (*Erythronium oregonum*): The white flowers of this 6-to-12-inch (15–30 cm) low grower nod down, but the petals curve upward, a characteristic typical of the lilies. The mottled, glossy leaves are also attractive, with their contrast of green and brown.

Chocolate lily (*Fritillaria lanceolata*, a.k.a. *F. affinis*): A name-rich native (a.k.a. rice-root lily, checker lily, mission bells), this bulb is a meadow must. Its purplish brown flowers, mottled with greenish yellow, hang down like the botanical equivalent of a fashionable flapper's cloche hat. Grows 1 to 2 feet (30–60 cm).

Western buttercup (*Ranunculus occidentalis*): Growing 12 to 18 inches (30–45 cm) tall, the buttercup provides a blast of bright yellow in spring through early summer. It is a familiar sight in the wild, attesting to its easy-growing nature.

White fawn lilies and broad-leaved shooting stars are a stunning combination in spring.

Satin flower (*Sisyrinchium douglasii*): This delicate flower blooms in early spring with reddish purple (and, yes, satiny-looking) flowers on 6-to-12-inch (15–30 cm) thin grasslike stems. Its other common name, grass-widow, seems too sad for this perky charmer.

Scotch broom, a nonnative scourge of Garry oak meadows, is a beautiful plant, but its effect on native habitat is deadly. To get rid of this scourge, Victoria broom-busting expert Eric Redekop offers the following advice: The best time to pull out broom is from October to January, when the soil is saturated with moisture and there's minimum soil disturbance from the pulling. Broom should never be pulled in the summer. However, the season of soil drought – from approximately mid-July to August, depending on the location – is the best time to *cut* broom plants. Stems cut below their first lateral root, under conditions of extreme moisture stress (i.e., drought), are least likely to resprout. However, stems cut above ground during the rainy fall and winter season are most likely to resprout. In other words, cut or pull depending on the season.

FROM TALL GRASSES TO BURSTING BLOOMS

ONE THING YOU get used to when visiting gardens: no matter when you arrive, people always say that you should have been there two weeks ago or waited two weeks. Basically, any other time is always better. But it wasn't modesty that prompted Pat Armstrong to say this when I visited her prairie garden in the Chicago suburb of Naperville in late July; it was the fact that Naperville had been declared a national disaster area the day before. Seventeen inches (43 cm) of rain had fallen in just 24 hours, and the place had been inundated. Soggy sofas, sopping carpets and drenched drapes lined the streets in great piles, waiting for garbage pickup, as we arrived to take in the grassland splendor of Pat's prairie garden.

Amazingly, only the small planting around Pat's mailbox seemed to have suffered from the flood, and squashed grasses were the sole testament to the water's torrential force. The rest of her one-third acre (0.13 ha) was perky and standing tall. I cannot imagine a more fitting tribute to the strength and resilience of the prairie. While all around us conventional plantings of typical suburban yards were gasping for life support, the prairie plants were saying, Catastrophe? We're built for catastrophe!

Consider the conditions under which prairies have evolved in North America: windswept acres and acres, with no arboreal shelter for miles; periods of prolonged drought and soaring temperatures; the killing cold of winter's blast; the crushing weight of bison herds and the accumulated chomping of thousands of nibbling grazers; the instant immolation by roaring, rapidly advancing fires. Not only have prairie plants survived such stresses, they positively depend on them as part of their health regime.

But tough as the prairie system is, it was not tough enough to withstand the depredations of plow and progress. Indeed, the story of the North American prairie is a narrative of loss. Native grassland communities once stretched from the edges of the great eastern deciduous forest to the Rockies. Now, they are highly endangered. In Canada, for example, less than 1 percent of the native tallgrass prairie of southeastern Manitoba and southwestern Ontario remains; less than 20 percent of the mixed-grass prairie and less than 5 percent of the original fescue prairie/aspen parkland ecosystems of Alberta, Saskatchewan and southwestern Manitoba remain; and only 30 to 50 percent of British Columbia's intermontane grasslands survive intact.

In the United States, similar statistics tell a story of loss. Estimates vary, but most experts agree that of the perhaps 400,000 square miles (1 million km²) of tallgrass prairie that existed in North America prior to European settlement, less than one-tenth of 1 percent remains. This is a staggering and sobering statistic – a numerical shorthand that cannot begin to encompass the wholesale destruction of this once dominant habitat.

Perhaps it is partly a problem of perception. When we hear the word *prairie*, we think of agriculture, great sweeping fields producing grain. And many of us think visual monotony, miles and miles of sameness.

The presettlement prairies of North America were landscapes shaped by native grasses, but they were by no means landscapes of monotony. Prairie

Previous spread: A prairie garden can look colorful and established after only a few years. This garden, started from seed just a couple of years ago, already seems to have existed forever. Wild bergamot (back left) and purple coneflower (foreground and back right) blend well with black-eyed Susan and blue vervain (middle). The tall shrub (back left) is red-osier dogwood.

forbs (nongrass, herbaceous – nonwoody – wildflowers) punctuated the grassy sea, offering explosions of color in spring, tall graceful wildflowers in summer and rich restful bronzes, golds, reds and purples in fall, as seed-heads matured. Even in the brutal prairie winters, the seed-heads stood sentinel, covered with snow, next year's promise of growth. The North American prairie was, above all, a place of diversity.

There are three broad prairie categories: tallgrass prairie, mixed-grass prairie and shortgrass prairie. On a map, the regions covered by these different prairies look something like long fingers seeping south. The tallgrass prairie, with its more abundant rainfall, is the most easterly prairie region. Extending even into a small section of southwestern Ontario, the tallgrass prairie has its most northerly expression in southeastern Manitoba (the Red River Valley) and follows a wide trajectory south into the midwestern states of the United States and on to the Gulf of Mexico. Typical grasses of the tallgrass prairie include big and little bluestem, Indian grass, switchgrass, prairie dropseed and sideoats grama.

The drier interior plains, from Saskatchewan and the western regions of the Dakotas to central Texas, are the mixed-grass prairie, where tallgrass and shortgrass species mingle or dominate, depending on site conditions. Grasses include blue grama, June grass, big and little bluestem and needlegrass. East of the Rockies, from southeastern Alberta and Saskatchewan to central Texas, where temperatures tend to be more extreme and rainfall less abundant, is the range of the shortgrass prairie. Buffalo grass, blue grama, hairy grama and sideoats grama can be found, along with tough, drought-tolerant forbs.

Although prairies are predominantly grassland ecosystems, each region has its associated woodland communities. In the east, for example, in areas where trees have taken hold, they tend to be oak woodland and savanna species, such as bur oak, post oak and shagbark hickory. Moving west, aspen parklands are plentiful in Alberta and Saskatchewan. And although we also tend to think of prairies as typically midwestern, British Columbia is dotted with prairielike intermontane grasslands (from Grand Forks in the south, through Vernon to Kamloops), and Washington and Oregon have gorgeous grasslands in the drier eastern regions.

Such sweeping characterizations cannot do justice to the tremendous variations within prairies, each of which has its own distinct character. Some sites

A remnant wild prairie, such as the Wolf Road Prairie in Chicago, Illinois, with its profusion of rattlesnake master, can teach us a lot about the native ecosystem on which prairie gardens are modeled. Dominant grasses include big bluestem, little bluestem, prairie dropseed and Indian grass. Common wildflowers include aster, black-eyed Susan, nodding onion, prairie phlox and obedient plant.

favor certain species and not others, some species lie dormant for decades, then explode in profusion, and each prairie changes over the years, responding to a host of factors about which we can only guess – these are the sorts of specific qualities that give different prairies their unique characters.

However, certain generalizations can be made, particularly with regard to how soil moisture affects the species of plants that survive in different prairie sites. In prairie areas with poor drainage, moist prairie species such as cord grass and swamp milkweed thrive. Mesic (or average moisture) sites with good drainage host a wide array of plant species such as big bluestem and compass plant. And on drier (xeric) sites with shallow soil, the truly tough bruisers thrive – the purple coneflower, leadplant and little bluestem, for example.

Fire has also played a crucial role in the development and maintenance of the prairies by keeping out invading trees and shrubs, warming the soil by exposing it to the sun so that the native warm-season grasses can flourish and recycling the accumulated nutrients in the thick surface litter, returning them to the deep, rich prairie soil.

Ironically, it was precisely this fantastic soil that led to the destruction of the prairies. Within just a few decades of settlement, the sea of native grasses had become a sea of cultivated plants, the basis for our agricultural economy – corn, wheat, oats, barley and rye, for example. The prairie sea became the Corn Belt. Even in those places not given over to agriculture, ecologically necessary rejuvenating prairie fires were suppressed, with the result that woody species and exotic weeds invaded and changed the prairies. Prairie grazers such as buffalo, pronghorns and prairie dogs, which helped to maintain the prairie system, were hunted and their populations drastically depleted before we even understood the ecological role they played. (It's estimated that in the late 1700s, 60 million buffalo roamed the central grasslands; in the early 1890s, the last wild buffalo was shot.) The wild denizens were replaced with domestic livestock, which have overgrazed and degraded the prairies. Nonnative pasture grasses were planted. Wet areas were drained. All of which led to a massive transformation, on a scale unequaled in North America.

Prairie wildflowers such as *Delphinium exaltatum* and sweet black-eyed Susan combine well in a sunny garden.

Identifying Prairie Natives

There are many good books about the ecology of prairie habitat and prairie-plant associations, including: *Grass Varieties in the United States* by A.A. Hanson (Washington: U.S. Department of Agriculture, 1972), *Grasses: An Identification Guide* by Lauren Brown (Boston: Houghton Mifflin, 1979), *Grasslands* by Lauren Brown (New York: Knopf, 1985), *Jewels of the Plains: Wildflowers of the Great Plains, Grasslands and Hills* by Claude Barr (Minneapolis: University of Minnesota Press, 1983), *Manitoba's Tall Grass Prairie: A Field Guide to an Endangered Space* by T. Reaume (Winnipeg: Manitoba Naturalists Society, 1993), *Manual of the Grasses of the United States* by A.S. Hitchcock (New York: Dover, 1971), *North American Range Plants* by James S. Stubbendieck, Stephan L. Hatch and Charles H. Butterfield (Lincoln, Nebraska: University of Nebraska Press, 1992), *Plants of the Chicago Region* by Floyd Swink and Gerould Wilhelm (Lisle, Illinois: Morton Arboretum, 1979), *Prairie Grasses* by J. Looman (Ottawa: Agriculture Canada, 1982), *Prairie Plants of Illinois* by John W. Voigt and Robert H. Mohlenbrock (Springfield, Illinois: Illinois Department of Conservation, n.d.), *Prairie Plants of the Midwest* by Russell R. Kirt (Champaign, Illinois: Stipes, 1995), *Tallgrass Prairie Wildflowers* by Doug Ladd (Helena, Montana: Falcon Press, 1995), *Wildflowers Across the Prairie* by F.R. Vance, J.R. Jowsey and J.S. McLean (Saskatoon: Western Producer Prairie Books, 1984), *Wildflowers of the Northern Great Plains* by F.R. Vance, J.R. Jowsey and J.S. McLean (Minneapolis: University of Minnesota Press, 1984) and *Wildflowers of the Tallgrass Prairie* by Sylvan T. Runkel and Dean M. Roosa (Ames, Iowa: Iowa State University Press, 1989).

But statistics don't tell the full story, for the prairie is also the site of some of the most energetic, community-minded and enthusiastic gardening activity on the continent. Nowhere did I find the phrase "native plants" rolling off the tongue with as much ease as in the Midwest. Nowhere did gardeners dive into debates about genetic provenance and seed-stock integrity with as much gusto.

There is a sense of urgency to prairie gardeners' efforts, a sense of optimism, a sense of mission – and a sense of humor. When you're trying to wean a whole culture off a landscape practice with huge ecological costs – the lawn – and replace it with an exuberant, sometimes unruly, always lively-looking landscape – the prairie garden – it helps to make the activity *fun*. (I even heard about a prairie planting on the *roof* of a house.)

Perhaps no group of gardeners has embraced this credo with more understanding of the transformative value of fun than the Wild Ones. Originally

A classic prairie combination of blazing star (front left), wild bergamot (back left), culver's root (back right) and butterfly weed (front right) lights up the garden with long-lasting blooms.

based in Milwaukee, Wisconsin, and with just nine members in 1979, the organization now has almost a dozen chapters and more than 1,000 members. The Wild Ones members are gardeners with a mission: "To educate and share information with members and community at the 'plants-root' level and to promote biodiversity and environmentally sound practices…in natural landscaping using native species in developing plant communities." And the plant community in their home range that has ignited their enthusiasm is the prairie.

What the Wild Ones offers members is a community of fellow prairie enthusiasts. It organizes annual natural-yard bus tours (and sitting surrounded by excited prairie gardeners on a sold-out tour, I thought I'd died and gone to naturalized heaven), practical workshops, "bulldozer alert" plant rescues and digs and "Help Me" days in which prairie gardeners offer advice to prairie neophytes. As well, its journal is a treasure trove of information and inspiration.

I was an anti-lawn raver well before I met the Wild Ones, but I wasn't prepared for the exhilaration I felt in the company of fellow anti-lawn fanatics. But communal agreement can't prepare one for the larger battle – most people love lawns. And the powers that be – the civic authorities, legislators and bureaucrats – will go to great lengths to defend lawns and repel any challenges to this dominant landscape aesthetic.

As a result, many Wild Ones members are walking encyclopedias of local bylaws, codes and regulations. They've had to learn the arcane language of legal restrictions in order to work the system, fight the system on its own terms or ferret out loopholes when necessary. But for those who eschew political battles, there is another course of action – the prairie garden: easy to maintain; gorgeous to look at; rooted, like the prairie grasses (some of which go down an astonishing 15 feet/4.5 m), in the past; gesturing to the future, a future in which the prairie sways again, in back and front yards across the continent.

When Rochelle Whiteman started her Glendale, Wisconsin, garden decades ago, her soil was pure clay, but with frequent additions of sand and compost, Rochelle solved the soil problem. An active Wild Ones member and a tireless educator on the environmental benefits of native plantings, Rochelle recommends that novice natural land-scapers start small – until they become obsessed, that is. Describing the process she went through to convert her yard to native plants, Rochelle says: "My neighbors watched me remove traditional evergreens – and cutting down the Norway maples *really* got their attention! – bring in loads of sand, build my own compost piles in various corners of the yard and experiment with earth-care practices, including smothering the periwinkle with cardboard and compost to transform areas in record time.

"My neighbors have changed some of their earth-care practices and have given up areas of lawn for other plantings. I believe they have come to enjoy the continuing *process* of gardening that goes on in my yard."

Pure Prairie

Naperville, Illinois

Pat Armstrong's garden is a faithful re-creation of the tallgrass prairie that once covered a vast area of North America. Here, yellow coneflower, wild bergamot (purple) and rosinweed (background, yellow) combine with grasses.

IT'S IMPOSSIBLE TO FEEL even a moment of doubt as to where exactly you are when you're at Pat Armstrong's place – you are right *in* the prairie. Every tiny detail, from the planting outside to the building materials of the house to the ornaments within, is connected to the prairie heritage of the place and to an active rejuvenation and restoration of that heritage.

Walking up the pathway to the house, one notices the prairie-grass profiles imprinted in the cement and the sandhill cranes painted on the garage door. Inside the house, images of prairie plants cover the walls, patterned in the tiles and wallpapers. Trilobite fossils decorate the coffee table. Standing in the kitchen, drinking a restorative glass of sumac lemonade – *Rhus* juice, as Pat calls it – made from the smooth or staghorn berries visible just outside the window, one also drinks in the possibilities of truly living, wholly and uncompromisingly, *in* a place.

"I'm not a gardener. I'm a nature observer," says Pat. But her words are belied by the magnificent garden, the one-third acre (0.13 ha) of tallgrass prairie in Naperville that she has nurtured. "I just put things in and observe what happens." Observe and celebrate, because "what happens" is a wonderful and diverse interplay of grasses, wildflowers and wildlife visitors. Pat has watched a provincially rare Cooper's hawk hunt in her yard, catching a mourning dove for breakfast. Additional sightings of box turtles, fox snakes, American toads, tiger salamanders, opossums and cottontail rabbits soften the blow of seeing a meal in action. At least 16 species of birds nest in her yard, and dozens more stop by for visits.

The reason Pat's yard is such a welcoming haven for creatures is clearly the vegetation: On a piece of property that harbored only one native plant when she bought it, there are now more than 140 species of prairie plants, 60 different woodland denizens, 20 species of trees, 20 species of shrubs and 20 different native grasses and sedges. (Twenty-two species are rare or endangered.) On any

Pat Armstrong planted an evergreen windbreak of juniper based on energy-conserving principles of design. As well, redbud and shadbush shelter the northwest corner of the house, and Virginia creeper climbs up the wall.

day between mid-May and mid-October, at least 30 species are in bloom. During peaks in July and August, more than 50 species are in full flowery flight. All this in one-third of an acre (0.13 ha).

It all started in 1983, after Pat's passive solar house had been constructed out of native stone and wood. First, she had a farmer plow the lot, then she seeded her limy clay soil with native grasses and wildflowers (everywhere, that is, except for a small woodland area, where a treasured bur oak stood). She kept an area close to the house as lawn, but it's a different kind of lawn: buffalo grass, a native adapted to prairie drought.

There have been many random changes during the past dozen or so years: The buffalo grass area has gotten smaller and smaller as prairie seeds arrive on the wind or courtesy of the birds; the sidewalk verge planting, originally only prairie dropseed and pale purple coneflower, is now resplendent with butterfly weed, vervain and Virginia mountain mint; the evergreen windbreak and shrub thickets of wild plum and dogwood have grown up enough to do their shielding energy-conserving good work; the Virginia creeper has also done service in the heat-conserving department, covering the house with a flush of green (and brilliant scarlet in fall); and the chinquapin oak seed planted in 1981 is now a 20-foot-tall (6 m) tree, clearly one of Pat's most beloved old friends. (Indeed, many of the plants have become personalized – the buffalo grass, for example, Pat endearingly refers to as cute little guys and gals, earning the accolade in mid-summer as it grows without a drop of water, while the neighbors' Kentucky blue is crankily calling for 2 inches/5 cm a week.)

Cranky attitudes were on my mind as I asked Pat about peoples' responses to her yard. She admitted that the people who don't like it are louder than the ones who do: Every year, the city gets at least one complaint, but every week, a handful of people stop by to tell Pat how much pleasure her yard provides. Perhaps the most satisfying response is from the little kids next door, who ask whether they can run through her paths after supper.

"I've restored the great-great-grandchildren of the plants that were originally here, when this land was prairie, before 1840," says Pat. A genealogy worthy of celebration and awe. And after-dinner scampers by the great-great-grandchildren of the land's other inhabitants.

Pat Armstrong's recipe for *Rhus* juice (a.k.a. Sumac Lemonade): Take one head of red berries from sumac (smooth sumac or staghorn sumac are best). Mash in a jug filled with cold water. Strain out the berries. Add 1 cup (250 mL) sugar. Enjoy.

PERHAPS AS A RESULT of the high-stakes battles that have been fought over prairie gardens, a number of myths persist in the polarized debate over replacing lawns with prairie plantings. And these myths tend to cluster around three hot-ticket items: weeds, work and wildlife.

First of all, weeds. Whenever someone throws out the weed challenge to me in a discussion about native-plant landscaping, I'm always tempted to retort: You tell me what a weed *is,* and then we'll talk. I imagine myself walking away, getting on with my life and returning, say, one year later to find the challenger still without an adequate definition. The simple fact is that there is no universal objective definition of weeds. Yes, there are weeds in specific circumstances: invasive nonnatives that colonize native habitats; plants (native or nonnative) that for whatever reason the gardener doesn't want in a specific spot; plants that interfere with a farmer's crops. Surely these are weeds. But they exist in a particular context. In another context, they may not be weeds. Take milkweed, for example. In a farmer's field, milkweed can certainly be a weedy problem. In an urban naturalized garden, on the other hand, that same species may be the only food within miles for the larval monarch butterfly.

If we do away with the notion of a universal definition of weeds, then we're left with situational practicalities and aesthetics. And on that score, each to his or her own, I say. Go to bat for your goldenrod if it's where you want it to be. Defend your deliberate plantings, and advocate for adventitious arrivals. Don't let anyone else dump *his* or *her* weed definition on *your* purposeful planting. (Unless, of course, the law is involved, in which case, pull 'em or prepare for a court case.) Tell those who object that you won't complain about their nonnative grass seed sprouting in your prairie if they pay you the same courtesy over your natives. Hope for détente.

One area of the weed debate in which détente is often not an option, though, is the subject of allergies. On that score, you'll likely need to resort to science. Print this slogan on your gardening t-shirt or stencil it on your garage door: *Goldenrod does not cause hay fever.* Add "scientists agree" or "according to all research on the matter," if you think there's any chance it will help to dispel

The line separating Pat Armstrong's exuberant prairie planting from the neighboring grass is a stark reminder that the prairie garden is still a relatively renegade aesthetic compared with the more common lawn landscape.

the myth that goldenrod causes hay fever. In my experience, rational discussion often encounters a sniffling red-eyed brick wall on this subject, but give it a try. Science is with you, even if the doubters aren't. As well, you can always point out that some of the most serious plant allergens are the ubiquitous nonnative grasses planted deliberately or invading lawns, such as Kentucky bluegrass, timothy, orchard grass and Bermuda grass – not the tallgrass prairie natives.

Another myth concerns work – specifically, the amount of work required to create a prairie garden. Unfortunately, a whole industry has sprung up around the idea of effortless sprouting – the meadow-in-a-can phenomenon. If you're interested in a true native meadow or prairie, a long-lived plant community of native grasses and forbs, these instant gardens in a tin just don't deliver. About the only thing they do deliver is heartbreak in year two or three, when the weeds take over after the first year's flush of colorful annuals. A thorough examination of the seed mix in five popular "wildflower" mixes, done by Pat Armstrong of Prairie Sun Consultants, revealed that these instant gardens are full of Eurasian, Mexican and European annuals, with precious few prairie natives.

You'll need to do a bit more work than flick your wrist. That said, however, prairie gardens (planted with appropriate seeds or seedlings, not the canned varieties) do tend to be a lot less work over the long term than conventional gardens or lawns. The key is that they're a lot *more* work in the short term. They demand excellent soil preparation – not in terms of soil amendments (which are generally not necessary) but in terms of preparing a clean, weed-free bed.

Proving that a garden's inspiration can come from surprising sources, Annette Alexander, whose mother and grandmother were both committed peace activists, says that the impetus for her prairie garden in Milwaukee, Wisconsin, was the Gulf War: "I realized that anything any one of us can do to heal the Earth in any place will help." Distressed by the high-energy consumption of lawn maintenance, Annette decided to rip out her grass and plant a prairie.

Because her garden is in a high-traffic area, Annette wanted it to look instantly attractive – all within a strict budget. She therefore started with a combination of seedlings and seeds. She gets wood-chip mulch, which she uses on the paths, free from the city, and found materials, such as logs and stumps, line the walkways.

(See Chapter 5 for details.) And once the prairie plants are in the ground, weed vigilance is crucial for the first few years. After that point, though, low maintenance is the name of the prairie game. But you'll have worked rather hard to earn that effortlessness.

Another work-related myth that needs pruning is the idea that prairie gardeners have just let their lawns "go." Nothing could be further from the truth. A lawn let go is simply that: a lawn let go. It's not a prairie garden. I'll go out on a limb here and confess that I think people should be able to do this if they want to (it's an interesting ecological experiment that will teach you a lot about weeds, disturbed landscapes and the nature of succession), but it's not a garden (at least not in the sense of a deliberately managed cultivated plot). And it's almost certainly not a native-plant garden. Unless you have about 150 years to spend on the experiment, the resulting landscape will be nothing like a "natural" landscape. Instead, there will be a lot of nonnative exotics. We've disturbed the landscape to such a degree and filled the soil with so many exotic seeds that ironically, it now requires an act of deliberate intervention to take the land back to anything near a "natural" state.

A simple design feature, such as framing an important view, will signal a well-thought-out plan in the prairie garden.

About that final myth – wildlife. A common but misplaced concern about prairie gardens is that they will somehow attract and harbor rats. Forget it. Rats are far more likely to forage in human garbage than in tallgrass gardens. You'll no more attract rats with your prairie dock than you would with delphiniums.

There's also great debate about mosquito populations in prairie landscapes, compared with conventional gardens. I must confess to being a bit of a fence-sitter on this one – a red-welted, uncomfortably scratching fence-sitter. I have never been so ravaged by mosquitoes as I was in the prairie wilderness of the West Chicago Prairie (though Cathedral Grove rainforest in British Columbia was a close second). On the other hand, it was a wild area, not a garden, and the summer was a particularly bad one for mosquitoes. Loads of prairie proponents, armed with studies, make light of the mosquito menace, pointing out that the insects breed in standing water, telling potential prairie gardeners not to worry because a prairie planting will actually absorb water faster than a lawn will. I think I'd agree with the not-to-worry part. I'd happily trade (and have done so often) a few more mosquito bites for the many more birds that feed on the insect life associated with prairie gardens. To my mind, the scary thing is the dead silence associated with lawns. Give me the birds and more bugs any day.

Randy Penner warns that his Winnipeg, Manitoba, prairie garden "looks messy to those people who prefer well-kept lawns," but it is part of a growing prairie movement to wean people off the perfectly controlled lawn look.

Randy has planted Manitoba natives of the tallgrass and mixed-grass prairie in an area of approximately 1,000 square feet (93 m²), with a ratio of half grasses and half forbs. But a bit of the prairie came with the house: When Randy stopped mowing his lawn, he discovered patches of big bluestem, which the previous owners hadn't planted.

Randy started in 1989 with a 10-by-9-foot (3 m x 2.7 m) test plot in the corner of his lot to see how the prairie garden would look. Happy with the results, he has since expanded the prairie coverage, mixing grasses such as Canada wild rye, little bluestem, blue grama and prairie dropseed with wildflowers such as culver's root, purple prairie clover, golden alexanders and smooth aster.

Although he purchased most of his prairie seedlings from local nurseries, Randy is particularly pleased with the three prairie species (blue-eyed grass, Canada milk vetch and wild pea vine) brought in and deposited as seeds by the birds and the wind. He now says that the garden "acts like a plant nursery, with seeds dropping in and coming up," not necessarily guided by a human hand.

Here, Randy's small patch of stiff goldenrod (yellow) and wild bergamot (purple) mixes with grasses.

Gorgeous Grasses for the Prairie Gardener

Aesthetic reconditioning – that's very often the process gardeners need to go through before they can appreciate the beauty of grasses. We're used to the splashy statements of colorful annuals and perennials, the loud lushness of ferns and groundcovers and the big boldness of trees and shrubs. But grasses offer grace. Nothing beats the gentle swaying of grasses in the wind or the subtle seed-heads and foliage golds and reds as summer ends.

And remember, too, all the good work that grasses do underground. The extraordinarily tough roots of deep-growing prairie grasses (on average, growing down in the soil 6 to 8 feet/2–2.5 m, compared with Kentucky bluegrass' 6 to 8 inches/15–20 cm) hold the soil, prevent erosion and help form that rich, fertile soil for which the prairies are famous. And above ground, they provide food and cover for ground-nesting birds.

(Unless otherwise noted, grow these grasses in full sun. And don't worry about drought. Most tolerate it, if not thrive in it.)

Wild Ones member and artist Lucy Schumann has done a wonderful illustration (available on Wild Ones t-shirts) showing prairie plants' aboveground and root structures. It's a graphic representation of why prairie plants are so tough: the fibrous mass of big bluestem roots, going down 9 feet (2.7 m); the thick carrotlike roots of compass plant, reaching down 16 feet (5 m); 16-foot-deep (5 m) liatris roots spreading out in a kind of river system of channels and meandering tributaries; and the gravital tug of white wild indigo's 11-foot-deep (3.3 m) roots plunging straight down.

In Kim Tyson's garden in Winnipeg, Manitoba, little bluestem forms a wonderful accent when planted in a half-barrel. Surrounding the grass are wildmint, northern bog violet and June grass.

Short to Medium-Height Grasses

Sideoats grama (*Bouteloua curtipendula*): This grass likely got its name from the oatlike seed-heads that grow on one side of the stem and droop and flutter in a very attractive fashion. This shortgrass, mixed-grass and tallgrass prairie plant grows 1 to 3 feet (30–90 cm). Average to dry soil.

Blue grama, a.k.a. mosquito grass (*Bouteloua gracilis*): Growing 1 to 2 feet (30–60 cm), this drought-tolerant grass of the mixed-grass and shortgrass prairie regions prefers dry, gravelly soil. Its fine leaves and attractive spikelets (almost like curling eyelashes), which bloom in late summer to fall, make this a fine garden addition.

Buffalo grass (*Buchloe dactyloides*): This mixed-grass and shortgrass prairie plant with grayish green foliage grows very low (to about 6 inches/15 cm) and thus makes a sensible alternative to nonnative lawn grasses. It flowers in summer. Tolerates clay soils; very drought-tolerant.

Crested June grass (*Koeleria cristata*): Blooming in late spring and early summer, June grass grows 1 to 2 feet (30–60 cm) with narrow, silvery green spikes at the end of leafless stalks. It is a grass of the mixed-grass and tallgrass regions. Dry, sandy soil.

Prairie dropseed (*Sporobolus heterolepsis*): This is my favorite grass. I agree with prairie-landscape expert Pat Armstrong, who describes its narrow leaves as creating a "beautiful fountainlike hummock." Fountain is right – prairie dropseed grass flows with grace. This tallgrass plant grows 1 to 2 feet (30–60 cm) and is especially useful as an edging plant. Its fine, narrow, bright green leaves turn bronze in fall. It blooms in late summer, and its seeds have a luscious scent. Moist to dry soil, clay to sand, but needs good drainage.

TALL GRASSES

Big bluestem (*Andropogon gerardii*): Justly prized as the signature plant of the tallgrass and mixed-grass prairie, this stately giant grows 6 to 10 feet (2–3 m) tall. It is also known as turkey foot because of its three-spiked seed-heads. Bluish green in summer, the grass turns a dazzling reddish purple in fall. A must in the prairie garden, for both its versatility and its beauty. Sun to part shade; wet to dry soil, clay to sand.

Little bluestem (*Andropogon scoparius*, syn. *Schizachyrium scoparium*): If your garden is too small for the tall-growing big bluestem, try little bluestem, which grows 2 to 3 feet (60–90 cm) and has attractive, fluffy, silverish seed-heads. Leaves turn reddish bronze in fall. Tolerates part

shade; prefers sand and well-drained average to dry soil.

Canada wild rye (*Elymus canadensis*): This tallgrass, mixed-grass and shortgrass prairie plant has a wide native range. Growing 3 to 5 feet (1–1.5 m), its dense seed plumes turn golden in mid- to late summer. Tolerates part shade; moist to dry soils, clay to sand.

Switchgrass (*Panicum virgatum*, a.k.a. *Dichanthelium oligosanthes*): Growing from 3 to 6 feet (1–2 m), this tallgrass prairie species has graceful leaves that arch and airy clusters of flowers and seeds in late summer. Leaves and seed-heads turn yellow in fall. It can be aggressive. Moist to dry soil.

Indian grass (*Sorghastrum nutans*): Another signature grass of the tallgrass prairie, Indian grass grows about 3 to 5 feet (1–1.5 m). Its seed-heads are silky tassels of gold-bronze in autumn, when the leaves also turn bronze. Tolerates clay soil, but prefers well-drained average to dry conditions.

Cord grass (*Spartina pectinata*): A tallgrass prairie plant for wet areas, cord grass grows 4 to 6 feet (1.2–2 m), with a graceful arching form and seeds that start out purply in summer, then turn yellow-gold in fall. Clay soil is fine, moisture a must.

Needlegrass, a.k.a. spear grass, porcupine grass (*Stipa spartea*): Growing 2 to 4 feet (60–120 cm), this tallgrass and mixed-grass plant has beautiful straw-colored leaves and silverish seed-heads in summer. It gets its name from its sharp-pointed seeds, which can hurt. Average to dry soil.

A mark of design prowess is the gardener's ability to use grasses well in a prairie planting.

SHRUBS FOR THE PRAIRIE GARDENER

Saskatoon (*Amelanchier alnifolia*); false indigo, a.k.a. indigo bush (*Amorpha fruticosa*); New Jersey tea (*Ceanothus americanus*); gray dogwood (*Cornus racemosa*); American hazelnut (*Corylus americana*); fragrant sumac (*Rhus aromatica*); smooth sumac (*Rhus glabra*); early wild rose (*Rosa blanda*); pasture rose (*Rosa carolina*); prairie rose (*Rosa setigera*); prairie willow (*Salix humilis*); meadowsweet (*Spiraea alba*).

When Shirley Froehlich and her family moved to their St. Andrews, Manitoba, home in 1987, the 1¹/₃-acre (0.5 ha) lot consisted of a summer-fallow field. Now, it is a showpiece of native-plant landscapes. There's a woodland, planted mainly with trembling aspen and a few green ash and white spruce, with shrubs such as smooth sumac, nannyberry and saskatoon around the edges.

Although many people worry about planting on top of septic beds, Shirley has had success with prairie grasses such as saline cord grass and switchgrass, which provide a sensible, low-maintenance alternative to traditional turfgrass.

Immediately around the house are the flowerbeds, originally all cultivated perennials but now mainly native prairie species. Here, culver's root (back left), Indian grass (middle), meadow blazing star (left and upper right), ox-eye (lower right) and upland white aster (middle left) provide midsummer color.

Shirley is the proprietor of Prairie Originals, a prairie native-plant nursery, so it is not surprising that her goal for the property is "to remove most of the lawn eventually and replace it with prairie plants."

STARTING OUT SIMPLE

The moisture-loving Queen of the prairie (bottom left) frames the tallgrass planting of ox-eye in Bret and Jina Rappaport's Chicago garden.

FOR BRET AND JINA RAPPAPORT, planting a prairie garden is all about "learning what we've forgotten." Bret calls himself a novice natural landscaper, and he's not afraid to ask questions or display his inquisitive spirit. As he says with a laugh, "I have to wait until stuff blooms to figure out what it is." On their one-

acre (0.4 ha) landscape in suburban Chicago, Illinois, Bret has learned a lot. He has experimented with various prairie planting techniques, discovering that for him, planting plugs into old-field grasses was a disaster compared with plowing and seeding or plowing and planting plugs. Now, five years after planting the prairie area with seed, he continues to experiment and enlarge the garden.

But Bret and Jina keep it simple. The prairie plants are all the generous and forgiving sorts, the kinds that reward one quickly with tall and floriferous abundance: bergamot, black-eyed Susan, butterfly weed, Canada goldenrod, compass plant, cup plant, fleabane, Joe-pye weed, ox-eye, purple coneflower, swamp milkweed, woodland sunflower. The only problem, said Bret, as we made our way on wood-chip paths through the head-high prairie, is that a few of these forgiving sorts are overly generous: The ox-eye, woodland sunflower and Canada goldenrod, in particular, are threatening to take over and will need to be held in check next year.

As part of their program to "keep it simple," Bret and Jina make do with the materials at hand. Found logs from the woodland at the edges of the property give shape to the garden paths. Plants are left to wander according to their inclinations. Gifts from other gardeners are accepted and tried out, wherever, whenever. And they take advantage of "Help Me" days offered by the Chicago chapter of the Wild Ones, when people who have been prairie gardening for years come by and offer advice to novices, providing answers and solutions to specific problems.

Though he counts himself among the crowd of novice natural landscapers, Bret stands out as a trailblazer in at least one very significant way: in his work as a lawyer and as national president of the Wild Ones, he paves the way (or, rather, unpaves the way) for natural landscapers everywhere, by fighting local weed and lawn ordinances, reshaping the dominant aesthetic and allowing renegade gardens such as his own to flourish and find a place in the suburban and urban landscape. He's helping plant the seed of a mass prairie movement.

The dazzling orange of butterfly weed looks stunning with blazing star – a drought-tolerant and low-maintenance prairie combination.

Native Wildflowers for the Prairie Gardener

The petals of the pale purple coneflower are narrower and more delicate than the brash blooms of the related purple coneflower.

PRAIRIE PLANTS ARE tenacious miracles of adaptation; the harsh conditions under which they evolved have ensured that ingenious survival strategies are bred right into their genes. One of the most fascinating projects prairie plants offer is a historical lesson in botanical evolution. By studying a plant's present adaptive mechanisms, the whole history of prairie evolution unfolds. Among these adaptations are deep taproots, which allow prairie plants to survive drought; the leathery roughness of prairie-plant leaves such as the silphiums and the hairy texture of plants such as pale purple coneflower are effective strategies for reducing the speed of the wind as it travels over the leaf, thus decreasing moisture evaporation. And some prairie denizens, such as the compass plant, orient the edges of their leaves north and south, thereby avoiding the full power of the midday sun on their large leaves – a trick of cool cunning.

The good news for prairie gardeners is that site characteristics which in any other context would be cause for hand-wringing – poor soil, drought, searing heat and frigid temperatures – are just business as usual for prairie plants.

At the opposite aquatic extreme, though, are those prairie plants adapted for moisture. A moist site, therefore, can offer the gardener a fortuitous opportunity, since so many of the moisture-loving prairie plants are stunning giants.

As if the above delights weren't rich enough, most prairie plants couldn't be showier or easier to grow. Any of the plants on the following list will reward you with effortless grace and a garden that looks mature and well lived in after just a few years.

Note: Invasiveness is a relative feature, but it's important to know that many prairie plants can become invasive or aggressive in the cultivated garden, where they lack the intense competitive pressures of the natural prairie. I personally approve of such speedy strength, but if you've got a small space, you may want to keep some prairie plants in check – weeding out seedlings, cutting back flowers before they go to seed and digging up volunteers and passing them along to other gardeners.

Spring-Blooming Natives for the Prairie Gardener

Pasqueflower, a.k.a. prairie crocus (*Anemone patens*, a.k.a. *Pulsatilla*): The white and purple flowers (large for the overall size of the plant) appear in early spring before the leaves, which are lacy and almost fernlike. Its stem is hairy, and its seeds are feathery plumes, rapidly dispersed by the wind. It grows 6 to 12 inches (15–30 cm). Needs good drainage.

Shooting star (*Dodecatheon meadia*): In some wild prairies, the spring explosion of shooting stars is a stunning sight. They carpet the moist earth with their pink to purple stars (often compared to cyclamen flowers), which hang down in profusion from leafless stalks. It grows 1 to 2 feet (30–60 cm) tall. Sun to part shade; wet to dry soil.

Prairie smoke (*Geum triflorum*): Another feathery low grower (6–18 inches/15–45 cm), prairie smoke has pink to purple flowers that hang down like bells, but it is the plant's wispy clumps of pinkish plumed seed-heads that make it a knockout. Sun to part shade; moist to dry soil.

Hairy puccoon (*Lithospermum croceum*): The leaves of hairy puccoon are fuzzy, hence the name. Flowers are golden yellow and appear in late spring. A low grower (10–18 inches/25–45 cm), it is good for dry sites in sun.

Prairie ragwort (*Senecio plattensis*): It's nice to have a yellow asterlike flower blooming in spring instead of in summer, when the prairie garden is full of such beauties. It grows to about 1 foot (30 cm). Sun; dry, sandy soil.

Blue-eyed grass (*Sisyrinchium angustifolium*): Grasslike narrow leaves and deep blue star flowers with yellow centers make this a delicate-looking plant. It grows to about 1 foot (30 cm). Sun; average to dry soil.

A stunning prairie combination: purple coneflower, black-eyed Susan, yellow coneflower, wild bergamot and, with its spiky white plumes, the incomparable culver's root.

Golden alexanders (*Zizia aurea*): Both the flowers (clusters of yellow appearing in late spring) and the seed-heads of this rapid spreader are very attractive. It grows 1 to 3 feet (30–90 cm). Full to part sun; moist to average soil.

Additional Spring Bloomers

Canada anemone (*Anemone canadensis*); alum root (*Heuchera richardsonii*); star grass (*Hypoxis hirsuta*); hoary puccoon (*Lithospermum canescens*); violet wood sorrel (*Oxalis violacea*); lousewort (*Pedicularis canadensis*); sand phlox (*Phlox bifida*); prairie buttercup (*Ranunculus rhomboideus*); wild petunia (*Ruellia humilis*); spiderwort (*Tradescantia ohiensis*); bird's-foot violet (*Viola pedata*); prairie violet (*Viola pedatifida*).

Joyce Powers of Mt. Horeb, Wisconsin, runs Praire Ridge Nursery and is a trusted source for many prairie gardeners. Her own garden, started from seed more than two decades ago in what was once a cornfield, now hosts more than 100 indigenous species. The purple flower is wild bergamot; the yellow flower on the right with drooping petals is yellow coneflower; the yellow flower on the left is black-eyed Susan.

SUMMER-BLOOMING NATIVES FOR THE PRAIRIE GARDENER
❧

Leadplant (*Amorpha canescens*): A leguminous semiwoody plant that fixes nitrogen in the soil, leadplant is a versatile prairie plant, with silvery foliage and dense purple flower spikes in early to midsummer. It grows 2 to 3 feet (60–90 cm). Sun; wet to dry, well-drained soil; drought-tolerant.

Butterfly weed (*Asclepias tuberosa*): Dazzling orange long-lasting flower clusters (this plant convinced me that orange has a place in the garden) in midsummer and its high value for butterflies make this a prairie must. It takes a while to get established because of its long taproot and resents transplanting. It grows 1 to 3 feet (30–90 cm). Sun; prefers dry, well-drained soil.

Canada milk vetch (*Astragalus canadensis*): This gorgeous plant has a lot going for it. It is leguminous, tolerates wet to dry soils and has beautiful spikes of creamy white flowers in midsummer that look a bit like lupines. It grows 2 to 4 feet (60–120 cm) and spreads rapidly. Sun.

White false indigo (*Baptisia leucantha*): Blooming in late spring and early summer, with white or creamy pea-like flowers, this legume also has attractive large seedpods. It grows 2 to 4 feet (60–120 cm). Sun; regular to dry soil.

Prairie coreopsis, a.k.a. stiff coreopsis (*Coreopsis palmata*): This rapidly spreading and exuberantly blooming plant sports yellow flowers in early summer and responds well to deadheading. Foliage is narrow and delicate and turns red in fall. It grows 1 to 2 1/2 feet (30–75 cm). Sun; average to dry soil; very drought-tolerant.

Pale purple coneflower (*Echinacea pallida*): A bit shorter than purple coneflower, growing 2 to 3 feet (60–90 cm), and with narrower petals, this is another easy-to-grow plant. Flowers are pale purple or dusty rose with dark centers. Great for birds and butterflies. Sun; average to dry soil.

Purple coneflower (*Echinacea purpurea*): Many prairie plants are almost effortless to grow in the garden, but purple coneflower is one of the easiest. It creates tall clumps (2–5 feet/60–150 cm) in almost no time, and seedlings will pop up all over the place. Large purple flowers with bright golden dome centers are long-lasting, appear throughout the summer and are showy at all stages. Moist to dry soil in sun to part sun.

Rattlesnake master (*Eryngium yuccifolium*): This unusual and highly attractive prairie plant produces stiff, spiny, bluish green leaves and utterly charming globe flowers, which are greenish white and last throughout the summer. It grows 2 to 3 feet (60–90 cm). Sun; wet to dry soil.

Flowering spurge (*Euphorbia corollata*): With its bright green leaves and small clusters of white flowers throughout the summer, flowering spurge lights up the garden. It grows 1 to 3 feet (30–90 cm). Sun; average to dry soil.

WINNING COMBOS

- black-eyed Susan, butterfly weed, pale purple coneflower, prairie coreopsis, prairie dropseed, spiderwort
- culver's root, prairie dock, wild bergamot, yellow coneflower
- flowering spurge, purple coneflower, showy tick-trefoil, wild bergamot, wild quinine
- culver's root, Michigan lily, ox-eye
- compass plant, rosinweed, vervain, Virginia mountain mint, wild quinine
- nodding onion, spiderwort
- black-eyed Susan, rough blazing star, stiff goldenrod, Virginia mountain mint
- butterfly weed, cylindric blazing star, flowering spurge
- butterfly weed, wild petunia
- evening primrose, purple coneflower, wild bergamot
- And for a sea of purple and white: flowering spurge, leadplant, rattlesnake master, showy tick-trefoil, vervain, white prairie clover, wild bergamot, wild quinine

It's easy to see why the leaves of prairie dock are sometimes called elephant's ears. In the outstanding wilderness area of the West Chicago Prairie, dock, culver's root and black-eyed Susan create a "prairie sea."

Ox-eye, a.k.a. false sunflower (*Heliopsis helianthoides*): This plant requires a warning, but it's a warning tempered with praise – it can be invasive. With its long-lasting, showy yellow flowers throughout the summer, ox-eye grows to about 5 feet (1.5 m) and creates dense stands. Sun; wet to dry soil, clay to sandy; highly adaptable. (Not to be confused with the nonnative ox-eye, or shasta daisy, *Chrysanthemum* x *superbum*.)

Rough blazing star, a.k.a. gay feather (*Liatris aspera*), cylindric blazing star (*L. cylindracea*) and prairie blazing star (*L. pycnostachya*): There are many striking blazing stars for the prairie garden. All produce showy spikes or wands of purple-magenta flowers in midsummer, and they last well, attractive even when they've gone to seed. All are great for butterflies, birds and bees. Rough blazing star grows 2 to 4 feet (60–120 cm) in dry soil. Cylindric blazing star grows 1 to 2 feet (30–60 cm); prairie blazing star has the showiest spike and grows 2 to 4 feet (60–120 cm) in average to wet soil, clay to regular.

Wild lupine (*Lupinus perennis*): The leguminous lupine sends up spikes of striking blue blossoms in early summer. The larval food source of the endangered Karner blue butterfly, wild lupine grows 1 to 2 feet (30–60 cm). Sun to part shade; average to dry, sandy soil.

Wild bergamot, a.k.a. monarda (*Monarda fistulosa*): Tubular lavender flowers shaped like a jester's hat are stunning, prolific and relatively long-lived, appearing in midsummer. Leaves are fragrant (like Earl Grey tea), and flowers attract bees, hummingbirds and butterflies. It grows 2 to 4 feet (60–120 cm) and spreads well. Sun; wet to dry soil.

Wild quinine (*Parthenium integrifolium*): I've seen this flower described as "insignificant," but I heartily disagree. Clusters of hard, knobbly white flowers (like tight little knots) are long-lasting in summer. It grows 2 to 3 feet (60–90 cm). Sun; wet to dry soil.

Purple prairie clover (*Petalostemon purpureum*): Perky is the word to describe this leguminous beauty. Small, purple flowers begin blooming in midsummer at the bottom of the flower head, and the head itself is large and thimblelike. Great for butterflies and birds, it grows 1 to 2 feet (30–60 cm). Sun; well-drained, dry soil.

Prairie phlox (*Phlox pilosa*): In early summer, the purplish rose flower clusters are showy. Leaves are hairy, giving

CLAY-BUSTING PLANTS

Prairie grasses and forbs adapt to a wide range of soil types – including clay. If you have heavy clay soil, don't despair. Plants that will do well (and, indeed, may grow taller on moist clay soils than on coarse dry soils) include big bluestem, black-eyed Susan, compass plant, cup plant, Indian grass, ironweed, New England aster, ox-eye, pale purple coneflower, prairie blazing star, prairie dropseed, purple coneflower, rattlesnake master, showy tick-trefoil, smooth aster, spiderwort, stiff goldenrod, switchgrass, wild bergamot, wild quinine and yellow coneflower.

the plant its other common name, downy phlox. It grows 1 to 2 feet (30–60 cm). Full to part sun; wet to dry soil.

Virginia mountain mint (*Pycnanthemum virginianum*): This member of the mint family (identifiable by the typical mint-family square stems) is delicate but attractive. Clusters of small white flowers appear in summer. It grows 2 to 3 feet (60–90 cm) in average to moist soil and can be aggressive. Sun.

Yellow coneflower, a.k.a. prairie coneflower (*Ratibida pinnata*): In midsummer (and sometimes lasting into early fall), the yellow flowers with drooping petals and cone disks are fantastic. Great for birds and butterflies, it spreads well and grows tall (2–5 feet/60–150 cm), though it tends to flop over if not supported by other plants. Sun; moist to dry soil.

Black-eyed Susan (*Rudbeckia hirta*): Depending on its mood, this plant sometimes behaves like a perennial, sometimes like a biennial and sometimes like an annual. But since it self-seeds like crazy, you'll have wonderful long-lasting yellow flowers with brown centers throughout the summer. Great for birds and butterflies, it grows 1 to 3 feet (30–90 cm). Tolerates part shade; moist to dry soil; prefers poor soil.

Compass plant (*Silphium laciniatum*), cup plant (*S. perfoliatum*) and prairie dock (*S. terebinthinaceum*): For tall, dramatic prairie plants, all the silphiums deliver, and each has distinctive, fascinating foliage. Compass plant gets its name from the way its leaves orient their edges to the sun. It grows 4 to 8 feet (1.2–2.5 m) in average to dry soil and produces showy yellow flowers in summer. Cup plant, which grows 3 to 8 feet (1–2.5 m), prefers regular to moist soil, though mine not only tolerates but is very aggressive in a dry site. (Be warned that this plant will take over.) Yellow flowers last throughout the summer and some years into fall. Leaves are coarse and grasp the stem, creating a moisture-holding cup. Great for birds and butterflies. Prairie dock is one of my favorites; its huge, almost rhubarblike basal leaves look stunning when the light hits them. It grows 3 to 8 feet (1–2.5 m), with bright

For a rich purple, pink and blue combination, blue vervain (middle and middle right), wild bergamot and purple coneflower are wonderful and easy to grow.

yellow flowers in summer, in moist to average sites. These silphiums all require sun and lots of room.

Blue vervain (*Verbena hastata*): It's a mystery to me why this plant is so underused in gardens. In summer, luscious blue flower spikes are showy and prolific. Blooms start at the bottom of the wand and progress upward. Growing 2 to 5 feet (60–150 cm), vervain spreads quite well. Sun; moist to average soil.

If you need an instant and attractive groundcover on a slope or berm, try wild strawberry (*Fragaria virginiana*) or common cinquefoil (*Potentilla simplex*).

Ironweed (*Vernonia fasciculata*): This stunner deserves a more enticing name. With showy clusters of brilliant purple flowers in mid- to late summer, ironweed grows 3 to 5 feet (1–1.5 m) and spreads well. Sun; prefers moist to regular soil, but mine does well in dry conditions.

Culver's root (*Veronicastrum virginicum*): Another stunner that deserves a home in prairie gardens. Its showy white flower spikes attract bees and appear in midsummer. Growing 3 to 5 feet (1–1.5 m) and sometimes floppy, culver's root prefers average to moist soil, but like the ironweed, mine is doing just fine in dry conditions. Sun.

Fall-Blooming Natives for the Prairie Gardener

Sky blue aster, a.k.a. azure aster (*Aster azureus*): Sky blue is right – this plant glows. Growing 1 to 4 feet (30–120 cm), it tolerates a wide range of soils, though it prefers sandy, well-drained soil. Sun. Smooth aster (*A. laevis*) is another blue beauty, and it grows on mesic or clay soils.

Heath aster (*Aster ericoides*): Airy white blooms cover this plant in early fall, just when the prairie garden has had enough of yellow for another year. It grows 1 to 3 feet (30–90 cm). Sun to part sun; dry to average soil.

New England aster (*Aster novae-angliae*): Every year, while trying to control my aggressive Canada goldenrod, I also pull out aster seedlings. I am then relieved that I've missed some when they turn out to be the stunning New England aster. Purple flowers appear in early fall and last well into the cold weather. It grows 2 to 6 feet (60–180 cm) and spreads well, but it can get floppy. Sun; various soil conditions, though it prefers moisture.

Fringed gentian (*Gentianopsis crinita*): With its striking blue flowers, each petal delicately fringed at the top, this biennial plant is a knockout. It grows 1 to 2 feet (30–60 cm) and needs moist soil. Sun.

Obedient plant, a.k.a. false dragonhead (*Physostegia virginiana*): Lovely spikes of lavender snapdragonlike flowers appear in late summer and last well. It grows 2 to 4 feet (60–120 cm). Tolerates part shade; average to moist soil.

Gray goldenrod (*Solidago nemoralis*): A somewhat more controlled plant than the common goldenrod, gray goldenrod is a wonderful addition to the fall garden, producing showy yellow flowers on 1-to-2-foot (30–60 cm) stems. It does not cause hay fever (ragweed does). Sun; dry soil.

Stiff goldenrod (*Solidago rigida*): The leaves of this plant are particularly showy – a nice bright green. Flower clusters are large, flat and yellow, at the top of 1-to-4-foot (30–120 cm) stems. Sun; a wide range of soils, from wet to dry, rich to nutrient-poor.

Fringed gentian provides a blast of blue in the fall garden.

Other Asters to Try

Smooth aster (*Aster laevis*); aromatic aster (*A. oblongifolius*); silky aster (*A. sericeus*); flat-topped aster (*A. umbellatus*).

It often surprises people to discover that southwestern Ontario is home to the tallgrass-prairie ecosystem, a landscape we tend to associate with the Canadian Prairie Provinces and the American Midwest. But at the time that 19th-century surveys were being carried out, prairies and open grassland savannas covered at least 205 square miles (530 km²) of southwestern Ontario, though now less than 0.5 percent of the original prairie ecosystem exists.

Larry Lamb is a Kitchener/Waterloo, Ontario, gardener who has done much work to educate, encourage and promote tallgrass-prairie gardening in southwestern Ontario. His own prairie garden, begun in 1985, serves as a wonderful example of what just one person with vision can achieve. In a typical suburban lot, surrounded by conventional grass lawns, Larry has faithfully re-created a bit of tallgrass-prairie growth, complete with a "bison-rubbing rock"!

A Prairie in Stages

Ringwood, Illinois

The informal path leading through Perle Olsson's 2½-acre (1 ha) prairie planting entices visitors to the woodland behind, which Perle likewise "gardens."

PERLE OLSSON TOLD ME that her golden retriever's call name, Maile, is the Hawaiian word for a sweet-scented flowering vine and that her registered name is Malagold's Tropical Storm. Maile lived up to both monikers as she roamed through the flowers. While I fretted at the incessant sounds of plants snapping and breaking, Perle shrugged and said, "If the prairie survived buffalo, it can survive Maile. What good is a prairie if dogs and other animals can't run in it?"

As Maile did her dog dance – racing, then suddenly changing direction, pouncing on bugs only she could see – Perle told me of her own philosophical dance: the dilemma of intervention. "Should I just let the plants go and find their own niche, or should I manipulate them?" It's a familiar dilemma but one uniquely acute in the native-plant garden. Mimicking nature, how far does the gardener go in accepting the fortuitous changes nature provides? "Should I pull them out? Should I let them stay?" are constant questions on Perle's mind.

In some ways, Perle's prairie garden is a lesson in the staying power of sneaky encroachment. Her 2½ acres (1 ha) began life as a lawn, and her husband, Karl, liked it that way. "There was no way in the world he was going to plow up his lawn, so I just kept taking out more and more." Bit by bit, Perle dug out patches and planted prairie seeds and plugs. In other places, she planted directly into the lawn. (Perle confesses to "hot arguments about mowing.") But slowly, inexorably, the prairie plants took hold, then spread their seeds, and now, the land is wholeheartedly, stunningly tallgrass prairie.

The neighbors, too, originally had objections, but Perle had sound responses to their concerns. Allergies? The bluegrass lawns of beloved convention contribute more to allergies than anything she's planted. Rats? They are more interested in human garbage than in the prairie. Her annual burn of the prairie? All done safely and with proper permit and notification procedures followed. Now, Perle's garden is a showcase for garden clubs, college classes and groups of neighborhood schoolchildren who come to visit and learn about the native landscape.

It's appropriate that Perle's garden is an educational gem, since she herself

A moist lowland area of Perle Olsson's garden provides the perfect conditions for this combination of Michigan lily (orange), ox-eye (yellow) and culver's root (white).

went through an intensive self-education process to bring the garden to its present glory. Her interest began more than 15 years ago, when she discovered a rare plant on her property – *Orchis spectabilis,* the showy orchid. She began to read up on plant communities, discovering which plants want to live together, which of the "wild" plants are native, which are nonnative; she learned the subtleties of her soil (the sand and gravel of the hill right through to the mesic areas and the low-lying wet places); then, in 1985, she began her planting experiments with seeds and seedlings.

At first, Perle confesses, her efforts looked "insane" – all those holes in the lawn, purple coneflowers in the bluegrass. But she was "renewed and inspired" every time she looked at the purple coneflowers. "Look at their legacy," she says. "They've spread all over. The prairie plants have overcome the bluegrass, even in places where I didn't pull out the lawn grass."

If sneaky encroachment is the secret, it's also sometimes a problem. The common milkweed, for example, is becoming a bit too aggressive on the top of the hill, and Perle thinks about pulling it, though milkweed is an important host plant for monarch butterflies. The Canada goldenrod, which came in on its own, is also taking over, and Perle suggests that prairie gardeners be careful with ox-eye, another take-over plant. But Perle's problems are few, and her design tips are sensible for any prairie planting: Put the short grasses in front, the taller grasses behind; plant new flowers close to the path for easy watering while the plants are getting established and so that young seedlings don't get lost in a mature planting.

But it was when Maile returned, her coat covered in flecks, that I recognized Perle's seed-collecting trick: Let the dog roam, as the buffalo once did, then comb her coat to harvest the next generation of prairie seedlings.

The elegant entrance to Perle Olsson's prairie signals that although the area may look wild, it is a well-loved, well-tended and purposeful planting.

Native Wildflowers for Moist Prairie Gardens

By now, it should be clear that "moist prairie" is not an oxymoron, although many people think of prairies as dry places. Wet prairies are indeed the home habitat for some truly spectacular species, many of which deserve a place in the home garden.

The following species all prefer moist sites, but if you've got regular conditions, give them a try. Chances are, they'll do just fine, perhaps not reaching the full extent of their stately height, but in the cultivated garden, this might be a blessing for some of these giants.

Swamp milkweed (*Asclepias incarnata*): This tall grower (4 feet/1.2 m) has beautiful clusters of dark pink to purple flowers in summer and a luscious vanilla scent. It is great for butterflies. Sun; tolerates regular garden soil, though prefers moist sites.

Spotted Joe-pye weed (*Eupatorium maculatum*): Joe-pye weed needs lots of space, with its dense clusters of fuzzy long-lasting pink (sometimes purple) flowers in midsummer at the top of 4-to-6-foot (1.2–2 m) stems, but rewards with a showy display. It is great for butterflies. Sun.

Common boneset (*Eupatorium perfoliatum*): Its leaves are somewhat coarse and hairy, but its masses of white flower clusters in summer make up for that. It grows 3 to 4 feet (1–1.2 m). Sun.

Queen of the prairie (*Filipendula rubra*): This tall grower (3–6 feet/1–2 m) produces dramatically showy clusters of pink flowers in midsummer. Sun; grows in average to moist conditions.

Bottle gentian, a.k.a. closed gentian (*Gentiana andrewsii*): There's no better blue in the garden than that of the bottle gentian in late summer and fall. The flowers are a fascinating shape – yes, like closed bottles – and the plant grows 1 to 2 feet (30–60 cm). Sun or part sun.

Sneezeweed (*Helenium autumnale*): In late summer, these prolific daisylike yellow flowers are a delight. Sneezeweed grows 2 to 5 feet (60–150 cm) and attracts butterflies. Sun.

Blue flag, a.k.a. wild iris (*Iris versicolor*): Blooming in early summer and looking like the nonnative irises, but without the beard, blue flag grows $1^1/_2$ to $2^1/_2$ feet (45–75 cm). Sun to part sun; moist but well-drained soil.

Turk's-cap lily (*Lilium superbum*): With its spotted, reddish, drooping flowers, this plant is a knockout, a dramatic addition to the moist garden. It grows 3 to 7 feet (1–2 m) and flowers in summer. Sun. Another lily for the moist garden is Michigan lily (*Lilium michiganense*). With its drooping, deeply curved orange flowers in summer, this tall grower (3–6 feet/1–2 m) likes rich soil in sun to part sun.

Cardinal flower (*Lobelia cardinalis*): You can't beat the brilliant red of this somewhat fussy flower. If it's happy, though, it will flourish. Just don't disturb its shallow roots. It grows 2 to 4 feet (60–120 cm) in sun or part shade and blooms in mid- to late summer.

Moisture-Loving Shrubs

Red-osier dogwood (*Cornus stolonifera*); swamp rose (*Rosa palustris*); prairie willow (*Salix humilis*); silky willow (*Salix sericea*); meadowsweet (*Spiraea alba*).

Queen of the prairie earns its royal moniker with its height *and* its showy flowers.

Queen of the Prairie

Milwaukee, Wisconsin

Lorrie Otto's prairie planting was at first vilified by local officials but is now such a mecca for visitors that a gravel pathway is necessary to accommodate the foot traffic. Lorrie sums up her philosophy of prairie gardening: "I'm going to celebrate Midwestern America, not take part in its homogenization."

I HAD MET DOZENS of Lorrie Otto's plant progeny before I met the woman herself. Many of the gardeners I visited in Milwaukee had one of Lorrie's plants in their yards and were eager to acknowledge the plant's special status – sourced right at *the* source of the prairie-garden movement in Milwaukee – Lorrie Otto's yard.

Few citizens can claim to have followed as dizzying a trajectory as Lorrie has. In 20 years, she has gone from a vilified thorn in public officials' sides to a celebrity with a day named after her in the City of Milwaukee.

Lorrie describes her yard as looking like a Christmas card when she moved in 45 years ago: 64 Norway and Colorado spruce trees and an acre (0.4 ha) of lawn. Lorrie had just begun the process of turning her yard into a native-plant sanctuary when a neighbor complained. A works crew arrived and cut down Lorrie's planting, transforming this once shy woman into a walking dynamo.

Imbued with that most compelling and disarming of traits – open-armed generosity – Lorrie is as quick to share her plants, her abundant knowledge and her infectious laugh as she is to share her opinions. But the opinions are radical, no-nonsense and refreshingly uncompromising. When I suggested that pet cats should be allowed out every once in a while, even if they do occasionally prey on birds, Lorrie responded with a statement which pretty well sums up her whole approach: "All those once-in-a-whiles add up. We can't have any more of those once-in-a-whiles." She'd also like to eradicate the North American lawn: "We all want beauty around us, so why settle for the lawn? Too many home-owners have been brainwashed by the spray people. They say things like, 'This yard is going to be insect-free by the end of the summer.' Well, that would be the end of the world."

Clearly, it's an environmental imperative that drives Lorrie's vision. An early and effective environmental activist, Lorrie planted her native garden on Earth Day in 1970. Lorrie tells me of one successful landscape experiment after another, seeing her garden as an array of "little laboratories." For instance, the sand-sandwich method of preparing the soil: dumping 3 feet (1 m) of leaves on top of the lawn, then 5 inches (13 cm) of sand, then leaves again and more sand. The raised area slowly settles and decomposes, creating a rich soil bed for seeds and seedlings.

Lorrie's garden has matured over the years with as much grace and vigor as she herself has. It's a showpiece of staying power, an example of all that can be accomplished if you just follow what you believe in. Who would have imagined when it all began that the woman who had to fight for her yard would one day be receiving accolades from Vice President Al Gore?

Rattlesnake master, with its yucca-like leaves and globe flowers, is an unusual-looking plant, but it demands little care and rewards with long-lasting blooms.

On the Wing in the Prairie Garden

Butterflies

Prairie gardens and butterflies are a perfect match. From larval food sources to showy nectar sources, prairie plants provide ideal habitat for a wide array of gorgeous butterflies, which feast in the sun.

Like finicky children, each butterfly species has a specific food requirement at its larval stage (though some, such as the painted lady, have a wide range of larval food plants). The only known larval food for the monarch butterfly, for example, is milkweed. The swamp metalmark, a threatened species in Wisconsin, lays its eggs only on swamp thistle leaves (and the loss of wetland habitat is thus having an impact on this butterfly).

In the adult stage, however, most butterflies will glean nectar from a variety of plants. To attract butterflies to a sunny garden, plant any of the natives listed on the following page. But remember, no pesticides, herbicides or insecticides (not even Bt) in the garden; they will kill butterflies.

A nectaring silver-spotted skipper on wild bergamot.

Birds

If you want to attract birds to your garden, any of the native wildflowers, shrubs and trees listed in this chapter are good choices. However, there are also a few general principles you should follow:

- Don't use any chemicals in the garden or on the lawn.
- Let your prairie grasses go to seed and remain uncut throughout the winter, thus providing food for the birds.
- Put in a birdbath.
- Plant berry-producing shrubs.
- Include some evergreen shrubs for winter cover.

The Canadian Wildlife Federation is conducting a coast-to-coast butterfly survey of species sighted in Canadian gardens. For more information, contact CWF, Butterfly Survey, 2740 Queensview Drive, Ottawa, Ontario K2B 1A2, or visit the CWF Web site: ‹http://www.cwf-fcf.org/surveys/butter.htm›. The University of Kansas, Department of Entomology, is coordinating a Monarch Watch, in which volunteers record sightings of monarch butterflies. For more information on monarch ecology, conservation and butterfly gardening, visit the Monarch Watch Web site: ‹http://www.keil.ukans.edu/~monarch/›.

BUTTERFLY LARVAL FOOD PLANTS

plant	butterfly
leadplant (*Amorpha canescens*)	dog face
Dutchman's pipe (*Aristolochia durior*)	pipevine swallowtail
aster (*Aster* spp.)	pearl crescent
wild indigo (*Baptisia lactea*)	orange sulphur, dog face
New Jersey tea (*Ceanothus americanus*)	spring azure, mottled duskywing
turtlehead (*Chelone glabra*)	Baltimore
showy tick-trefoil (*Desmodium canadense*)	eastern tailed blue, hoary edge
spicebush (*Lindera benzoin*)	spicebush swallowtail
wild lupine (*Lupinus perennis*)	Karner blue, silvery blue
wild petunia (*Ruellia humilis*)	buckeye
blue vervain (*Verbena hastata*)	buckeye
ironweed (*Vernonia fasciculata*)	American painted lady
violet (*Viola* spp.)	great spangled fritillary, meadow fritillary

BUTTERFLY NECTAR SOURCES

Wildflowers: giant hyssop (*Agastache* spp.); wild onion (*Allium canadense*); pearly everlasting (*Anaphalis margaritacea*); dogbane (*Apocynum androsaemifolium*); milkweed (*Asclepias* spp.); aster (*Aster* spp.); Canada milk vetch (*Astragalus canadensis*); boltonia (*Boltonia asteroides*); partridge pea (*Cassia fasciculata*); New Jersey tea (*Ceanothus americanus*); coreopsis (*Coreopsis* spp.); purple coneflower (*Echinacea purpurea*); fireweed (*Epilobium angustifolium*); fleabane (*Erigeron annuus*);

rattlesnake master (*Eryngium yuccifolium*); common boneset (*Eupatorium perfoliatum*); bluestem Joe-pye weed (*Eupatorium purpureum*); snow-on-the-mountain (*Euphorbia marginata*); Queen of the prairie (*Filipendula rubra*); sneezeweed (*Helenium autumnale*); sunflower (*Helianthus* spp.); ox-eye (*Heliopsis helianthoides*); blazing star (*Liatris* spp.); puccoon (*Lithospermum* spp.); cardinal flower (*Lobelia cardinalis*); bee balm (*Monarda didyma*); wild bergamot (*Monarda fistulosa*); purple prairie clover (*Petalostemon purpureum*); phlox (*Phlox* spp.); Virginia mountain mint (*Pycnanthemum virginianum*); yellow coneflower (*Ratibida pinnata*); black-eyed Susan (*Rudbeckia hirta*); wild petunia (*Ruellia humilis*); cup plant (*Silphium perfoliatum*); goldenrod (*Solidago* spp.); spiderwort (*Tradescantia ohiensis*); vervain (*Verbena* spp.); violet (*Viola* spp.).

PLANTS TO ATTRACT HUMMINGBIRDS

With their long bills and tongues, hummingbirds are perfectly equipped for sourcing nectar, and they are voracious feeders, reputedly requiring more than 100,000 calories a day.

Wildflowers: yellow giant hyssop (*Agastache nepetoides*); wild columbine (*Aquilegia canadensis*); butterfly weed (*Asclepias tuberosa*); Canada milk vetch (*Astragalus canadensis*); trumpet creeper (*Campsis radicans*); wild senna (*Cassia hebecarpa*); Indian paintbrush (*Castilleja coccinea*); turtlehead (*Chelone glabra*); purple coneflower (*Echinacea purpurea*); spotted Joe-pye weed (*Eupatorium maculatum*); jewelweed (*Impatiens* spp.); cardinal flower (*Lobelia cardinalis*); trumpet honeysuckle (*Lonicera sempervirens*); wild bergamot (*Monarda fistulosa*); lousewort (*Pedicularis canadensis*); beardtongue (*Penstemon digitalis*); phlox (*Phlox* spp.); obedient plant (*Physostegia virginiana*).

Neighbors

When it comes to accepting the different aesthetic quality of prairie gardens in the urban setting, we're at a confusing cusp. On the one hand, enlightened parks departments, transportation officials, school-ground administrators, conservation organizations and, of course, home gardeners are encouraging prairie plantings wherever there's a patch of land ripe for restoration. On the other hand, some neighborhood groups and municipal officials are fighting this trend.

The homeowner who decides to "go native" is often confronted with a bewildering array of laws, regulations, requirements and, sometimes, outright hostility. In the United States, for example, even though the federal government, through an Executive Memorandum issued by President Clinton in 1994, recommends the use of native plants on federally funded landscape projects, the gardener is still likely to encounter neighborhood opposition. And in Canada, many communities have height-restriction bylaws for plantings, which can be used against prairie gardeners.

It is therefore at the back fence or on the sidewalk that prairie gardeners need to hone their persuasive powers – either that or let the plants do it for them by creating landscapes of such beauty that nobody offers a peep of dissent.

There are a number of steps that prairie gardeners can take to prepare the neighborhood for the landscape changes which are about to occur. The main thing, I find, is to be *present*. Nothing disarms opposition more effectively than a show of dirty hands and committed digging. Let your neighbors know, simply by your presence in the garden, that your land is being cared for, that this is a purposeful project, that there's nothing delinquent about your landscaping efforts. Talk with your neighbors. Tell them of your prairie hopes, dreams and vision. Tell them of your plan – its timetable, your realistic goals and expectations. At the tiniest shred of interest, offer them plants – be generous. Not only is there strength in numbers and less chance of opposition, but shared enthu-

Perhaps the most persuasive way to disarm prairie opposition is to invite neighbors over to enjoy the prairie-garden experience.

siasm is one of the main ways that prairie gardening is going to take hold in neighborhoods across the region.

One of my favorite stories of shared enthusiasm is that of Becky Rush and her husband of Grafton, Wisconsin. According to the Wild Ones journal, they invited their neighbors over for an evening of slides and socializing before they began their naturalized garden. The result: All the new owners in the neighborhood began considering a similar landscape.

In addition to talking with your neighbors, learn everything you can about bylaws, weed ordinances, height restrictions and the like. For example, some communities mandate buffer zones around prairie plantings. Property lines and sidewalks must be surrounded by low growth even if there's tallgrass growth in the middle of the yard. Other communities require that prairie gardeners apply for a permit; and in some communities, permits will be granted only if at least 51 percent of the property owners in the immediate vicinity approve the application. Still others don't care as long as local weed ordinances are respected and there are no plants present that are listed as noxious weeds (often nonnatives anyway, and therefore not likely to be included in the prairie garden). And then there are those few truly visionary places, such as Long Grove, Illinois, that actually *encourage* people to plant native gardens. We're still a long way from this as the norm, but every effort you make to communicate with neighbors and local officials about the ecological benefits of prairie gardens will move us collectively closer to this goal.

I'm not much of a fan of the fence or mowed-border approach to prairie plantings (if it's mandated, that is; if it's a personal choice, then I'm all for it), but I do like the idea of signage, mainly for its inspirational and educational value. I'm convinced that some of the people who now grumble on their way past prairie gardens would perk up – and quite possibly have their interest so piqued that they would consider doing their own plantings – if there were simply a small sign, something marking the place as special.

Many people have made their own signs, but two organizations also sell them: the Wild Ones and the National Wildlife Federation.

My favorite sign is one I saw in Green Bay, Wisconsin. On a vacant lot that Peach and Tom Robinson are restoring to prairie, there's a hand-painted sign that reads: "Do Not Mow: Wild Flowers and Land Mines!"

People Power in Prairies

West Chicago Prairie, Illinois

Blazing star (purple), culver's root (white spikes) and rattlesnake master (white globes) in the West Chicago Prairie.

EVERY WILD AREA needs someone like Mel Hoff, president of a group of volunteer stewards of the West Chicago Prairie. After spending a magnificent day up to my neck in that moist prairie's tall grasses and forbs – all of us emerging from the walk with different watermarks on our clothes – I realized that I'd never before met anyone who knows every square inch of soil as well as Mel knows that wild prairie.

What Mel and his group are doing is gardening on a grand and urgent scale. He jokes about the prairie being his "semiprivate garden," and what I take him to mean is that he's doing what every gardener does: stewarding a piece of land. But his landscape practice diverges from that of most conventional gardening: Mel is directed in his "garden" not by any preconceived notions of what *he* wants it to look like but by what the prairie itself wants to *be*. This is stewardship in its most humble and respectful expression.

With a volunteer core of 150 to 175 people (about 75 of whom come out to two or more workdays), Mel and his stewards collectively spend roughly 3,000 person-hours a year looking after the West Chicago Prairie. (With over 550 species of flowering plants in 305 acres/123 ha, the West Chicago Prairie is one of northern Illinois' premier prairie areas.) They do restoration plantings, sometimes with school groups, and have devised ingenious methods for animating the kids' interest in the prairies; while collecting seeds, for instance, Mel sends children off to look for "fuzzy hotdogs," a.k.a. blazing star.

The volunteers lead tours of the prairie, sharing their conservation ethic with others. They advise county officials on prairie-management practices. (Mel hopes that the volunteer stewards will be allowed to do the ecologically necessary prairie burn, for which the officials just don't have the resources.) They do botanical inventories and map the prairie, noting changes, improvements and problems. They control encroaching nonnatives and those natives, such as gray dogwood, which are taking over in the absence of fire. They collect and sprout seedlings (Mel speculates that there's something genetic which makes this kind of foraging so satisfying to humans) and restore degraded areas of the prairie using this indigenous seed stock. (There was hardly enough room for Mel's car in the garage when I visited, full to the brim as it was with seeds and hulls.) And in a symbolic act with deep resonance, they give names to sections of the prairie – wolfberry prairie and three-oak prairie, for example – so that everyone will know that this land is truly valued and tended, gardened in the most caring way.

For more information on the volunteer stewardship program, which looks after numerous prairie sites in the United States, contact The Nature Conservancy (8 South Michigan, Suite 900, Chicago, Illinois 60603), local county or state nature-preserve districts or your state Department of Natural Resources. For information on Canadian prairie initiatives, contact the Rural Lambton Stewardship Network (P.O. Box 1168, 1023 Richmond Street, Chatham, Ontario N7M 5L8) or the Manitoba Naturalists Society (401-63 Albert Street, Winnipeg, Manitoba R3B 1G4).

Almost Instant Elegance

Western Springs, Illinois

With its thimblelike flower head, purple prairie clover *glows*.

WHILE HELEN VANDENBERG'S backyard prairie garden obviously gives her a lot of pleasure, perhaps the biggest pleasure belongs to her neighbor. Helen's is the first (and so far only) garden I've seen that caused an architectural about-face in the neighborhood. When a neighbor was adding a second-floor addition, the architect specified no north-facing windows. But the neighbor insisted…Helen's prairie garden was the view, and it was a view the neighbor did not want to miss.

Designed by Pat Armstrong, planted and maintained by Helen, this prairie garden is composed entirely of Illinois natives and shows just how magnificent an average-sized backyard can be. And just how quickly that magnificence can come about.

The year before planting, in 1993, the lawn was covered with black plastic. Then, over the dead grass, Pat and Helen put layers of newspaper (five sheets thick) and brought in a truckload of dirt (unfortunately full of thistle seed – a problem that led to much weeding initially). Into the bed, Helen first placed plugs of prairie forbs following Pat's design, an ovoid shape with the tallest plants in the center. These seedlings were mulched to conserve moisture and keep out weeds. Then Helen seeded the grasses – prairie dropseed, which in places forms a band around the perimeter of the garden, sideoats grama, big and little bluestem, June grass. The young planting was kept well watered that first year until August, when Helen stopped watering to encourage deep root development. Now, the drought-tolerant plants require no supplemental watering.

The ratio of forbs to grasses was about 50:50 at the outset, and both Pat and Helen recommend the use of seedlings for the forbs and seeds for the grasses. This leads to a high success rate with the forbs and also to an almost instant show.

The garden was just three years old when I saw it, but it looked as if it had been there forever – something I suspect Helen's neighbors think every morning as they peer into the prairie sea.

Helen Vandenberg's Western Springs, Illinois, prairie garden, designed by Pat Armstrong, is a dazzling change from the lawn that once covered the whole backyard.

It probably makes the most sense to begin by cataloging the things that John Shankland's prairie garden in La Grange, Illinois, does *not* have going for it: It has the notoriously allelopathic black walnut tree under which many plants die, too much shade and a gardener who would prefer not to garden. But what the garden very definitely has going for it is John's deep love of the prairie and his desire to nurture a small bit of prairie growth in his backyard.

With little maintenance other than a sneaky burn every few years (done with the neighbors' collusion) and a fall weed-whacking in nonburn years, John's backyard prairie is testament to the tough staying power of prairie plants.

INVASIVE ALIENS

When I became interested in native-plant gardening, I never thought that I would be able to learn and remember the Latin names of the plants I was growing. It didn't bother me, and I didn't set myself the goal of learning botanical Latin, but nevertheless, the information seeped through my thick memory block until I can now mangle Latin pronunciations with the best of them.

It's the same with keeping track of which plants are natives and which are aliens. At first, it seemed hopelessly daunting to think that I could retain a running inventory at all times. But as one becomes familiar with native-plant communities in the wild, it becomes increasingly obvious which plants are native and which are aliens. First of all, the alien species usually behave differently. Very often, they create dense monocultures. As well, they tend to cluster around disturbed habitats and waste places or at the edges of wild areas.

The main thing to remember is that just because a plant is growing in the wild does not mean it's a native. Examples of very familiar nonnatives – introduced alien species that now grow so commonly in the wild or in disturbed areas that many people mistake them for natives – include: bachelor's-button, butter-and-eggs, Canada thistle, catnip, chicory, curly dock, dame's rocket, dandelion, daylily, nightshade, orange hawkweed, ox-eye or shasta daisy, plantain, purple loosestrife, Queen Anne's lace, spearmint, tall buttercup, tansy, teasel, yellow flag.

While many naturalized alien plant species do little in the way of ecological harm, some have become severe threats to plant communities in the wild. What they mainly do is outcompete natives, creating a dense monoculture, infesting and spreading at the expense of native-plant diversity. And many of these invasive aliens are very difficult to control. One fellow who has done an inventory of invasive aliens in the Milwaukee County Park System calls his effort the Sisyphus Project, which says it all.

The following invasive exotic species should *not* be planted near wild prairie areas. If they appear, they should be pulled.

Herbaceous Plants: garlic mustard (*Alliaria officinalis*); ox-eye or shasta daisy (*Chrysanthemum* x *superbum*); Canada thistle (*Cirsium arvense*); field bindweed (*Convolvulus arvensis*); crown vetch (*Coronilla varia*); leafy spurge (*Euphorbia esula*); creeping Charlie (*Glechoma hederacea*); dame's rocket (*Hesperis matronalis*); purple loosestrife (*Lythrum salicaria*); white sweet clover (*Melilotus alba*); yellow sweet clover (*Melilotus officinalis*); Japanese knotweed (*Polygonum cuspidatum*).

Grasses: quack grass (*Agropyron repens*); smooth brome (*Bromus inermis*); reed canary grass (*Phalaris arundinacea*); Johnson grass (*Sorghum halepense*).

Vines: Oriental bittersweet (*Celastrus orbiculatus*); Japanese honeysuckle (*Lonicera japonica*); kudzu (*Pueraria lobata*).

Shrubs: Japanese barberry (*Berberis thunbergii*); autumn olive (*Elaeagnus umbellata*); Amur honeysuckle (*Lonicera maackii*); tatarian honeysuckle (*Lonicera tatarica*); common buckthorn (*Rhamnus cathartica*); glossy buckthorn (*Rhamnus frangula*); multiflora rose (*Rosa multiflora*); European highbush cranberry (*Viburnum opulus*).

Trees: Norway maple (*Acer platanoides*); tree of heaven (*Ailanthus altissima*); Siberian elm (*Ulmus pumila*).

For more information on the problems and control of invasive alien species, contact the Natural Areas Association (108 Fox Street, Mukwonago, Wisconsin 53149) for a copy of *The Natural Areas Association Compendium of Exotic Species* or the Canadian Wildlife Service for *Invasive Plants of Natural Habitats in Canada* (Habitat Conservation Branch, Environment Canada, Ottawa, Ontario K1A 0H3). The Brooklyn Botanic Garden has also published an informative guide, *Invasive Plants: Weeds of the Global Garden* by John Randall and Janet Marinelli.

FROM TOWERING WOODLANDS TO SUNNY MEADOWS

TORONTONIANS MAY (I hope) be forgiven if we sometimes sound as though we *think* we live at the center of the universe. Of course, it's not the case, but perhaps a certain degree of hubris is inevitable when, as *is* the case, one can look out from the top of Toronto's CN Tower and see the home habitat of one-fifth of the population of Canada and the humming center of Canada's financial market.

The view from the CN Tower also reveals the price we pay for our position. From this perch, we can see once clean Lake Ontario reduced to an unswimmable, unfishable, undrinkable state (without massive "purification" treatment, that is). We can see the industries that pour waste into this seemingly endlessly forgiving body of water – though that forgiveness is an illusion created by our lack of investigation into what actually occurs as a result of such dumping. We can see the industrial stacks reaching high into the sky, pumping out puffs of…what exactly *are* those white clouds, anyway? We can even see the open flames on the Hamilton industrial shoreline. And where we could once see farmlands and forests and wetlands, we can increasingly see new housing developments, new highway corridors, new settlements popping up to feed the demands of a growing population base.

The *land* itself seems to be literally disappearing. Favorite nooks and crannies of undeveloped, almost secret caches go the way of development with growing regularity. Lose sight of a favorite wetland, then return a year later, and often it's gone, with a sign heralding "Marsh Corner Housing Estate" in its place. It's almost as if our goal for the region were complete concretization, complete erasure of the natural features that, after all, made this place so desirable for settlement in the first place. This is one of the central ironies of the Great Lakes region: We're destroying precisely those features which make it function as a healthy, lively place like no other.

But, of course, all is not bleak. Despite the dizzying demands of rapid development, the Great Lakes region is still an area of unparalleled beauty. The monarch butterflies return by the millions year after year and, in the fall, gather in great profusion by the shores of Lake Erie to begin their southern migration. The bird activity at Point Pelee is legendary, a mecca for bird aficionados across the continent. Indeed, Point Pelee becomes a kind of human migration stop for bird watchers in the spring and fall.

And all this wildlife activity is not restricted to nonurban places. Even in the middle of downtown Toronto, Canada's largest city, coyotes can sometimes be heard, howling hauntingly on summer nights in the Don Valley.

The northeastern region of the United States and the somewhat less urbanized corridor spreading east of the Great Lakes in Canada are also areas in which the demands of development are creating an uneasy truce between human populations and wild populations of plants and animals. Though there are countless oases in the midst of such pressures, the Northeast is a region of

Previous spread: At his cottage near Peterborough, Ontario, Jim French has created a spectacular woodland garden using colorful natives such as trilliums (pink and white) and Virginia bluebells (blue).

intense settlement as cities spread their tentacles into the surrounding countryside.

Though northern New England, with its characteristic hardwood forests and mountainous areas, is generally less populated than warmer southern New England, with its oak-hickory forests, one can read throughout the region traces of human impact on the land: marshes and ponds once so abundant in southern New England now being drained and "improved" for subdivisions; the dry sand plain and pine-barren communities of southern New England, New Jersey, Long Island and Cape Cod in increasing demand as vacation spots....

But surrounded by proof of nature's tenacity, dwellers in these regions have begun to value, protect and restore the unique natural features that give the area its character and identity: its broad-leaved deciduous forests of maple, beech, oak, elm, ash and birch; its productive marshes and wetlands; its forest clearings full of sunny-meadow forbs and grasses.

Northeastern woodland gardens are often imbued with a sense of calm. A spongy moss cover can create this soothing effect, while the wild blue phlox in the background provides a splash of color in spring.

Naturalization groups have popped up in the region like goldenrod in a clearing, working on re-greening school grounds, revitalizing creeks and whole watersheds, lobbying for increased protection of existing wild areas, doing the backbreaking work of clearing out invasive exotic species that are threatening forests, and much more.

And working behind the scenes, sometimes in hidden backyards, sometimes in declarative front yards, are the thousands of gardeners using native species. Whether it's a hesitant novice planting a native species here and there or a full-scale naturalization effort – someone attempting to re-create a fully functioning ecosystem – a great deal of native-plant gardening is going on in the region.

There are many different approaches to the use of native plants and no *one* right way. Just a single wild bergamot plant, tentatively purchased by a curious soul and added to a bed of exotics, will offer nectar to butterflies, bees and

The appearance of bloodroot announces spring. Though the flowers are fleeting, the leaves make it an ideal groundcover.

hummingbirds and seeds to birds and will perhaps inspire that curious soul to try other natives. Pretty soon, that tentative gardener will be making more and more space for natives, seeing how relatively effortlessly some of them grow, admiring their forgotten and neglected beauty, becoming convinced that natives deserve pride of place in the garden. Native-plant gardening is all about taking down the fence (metaphorically, not necessarily literally) that separates the wild from the tame; it's all about making a place for wildness in our lives, becoming a part of that wildness, in fact.

Here, then, are profiles of a few native-plant gardeners in the Great Lakes, northeastern, mid-Atlantic and eastern Canada regions who have renegotiated the boundary between wild and tame, who have gone a little wild in their lives and are happy to share the results of their efforts. Here, too, are dozens of wonderful native plants for gardeners in these regions.

IDENTIFYING NATIVES

Along with the excellent Peterson and Audubon field guides to wildflowers, there is a plethora of regional and local guides to the flora of the Great Lakes, northeast, mid-Atlantic and eastern Canada – too many to list. A quick look at any local library or bookstore or an inquiry to a local naturalist group will get you started.

Good general guides to the ecology of the region include: *Deciduous Forests of Eastern North America* by E. Lucy Braun (New York: Free Press, 1974), *Eastern Forests* by Ann Sutton and Myron Sutton (New York: Knopf, 1993), *A Field Guide to Ecology of Eastern Forests* by John C. Kricher and Gordon Morrison (Boston: Houghton Mifflin, 1988), *Forests: A Naturalist's Guide to Trees and Forest Ecology* by Lawrence C. Walker (New York: Wiley, 1990), *A Guide to New England's Landscape* by Neil Jorgensen (Chester, Connecticut: Pequot Press, 1977),

Handbook of the Trees of New England by Lorin Dame and Henry Brooks (New York: Dover, 1972), *The Plant Explorer's Guide to New England* by Raymond Wiggers (Missoula, Montana: Mountain Press, 1994), *A Sierra Club Naturalist's Guide to the Middle Atlantic Coast* by Bill Perry (San Francisco: Sierra Club Books, 1985), *A Sierra Club Naturalist's Guide to the North Atlantic Coast: Cape Cod to Newfoundland* by Michael Berrill and Deborah Berrill (San Francisco: Sierra Club Books, 1982), *A Sierra Club Naturalist's Guide to the North Woods* by Glenda Daniel and Jerry Sullivan (San Francisco: Sierra Club Books, 1981), *A Sierra Club Naturalist's Guide to Southern New England* by Neil Jorgensen (San Francisco: Sierra Club Books, 1978) and *Trees: An Introduction to Trees and Forest Ecology for the Amateur Naturalist* by Lawrence C. Walker (Toronto: Prentice-Hall, 1984).

Jim Hodgins, the editor of *Wildflower* magazine and coauthor of *Flowers of the Wild*, is highly knowledgeable about native flora, but he began his Toronto, Ontario, garden by asking the same questions that any naturalistic gardener faces: What kind of habitat does my garden *want* to be? What indigenous plant community makes ecological sense in this place?

Jim's garden is modeled on the maple-beech forest community that once covered much of the Toronto region. In a tiny space (approximately 15 feet/4.6 m square), Jim has planted hundreds of diverse woodland species and many shrubs and trees, such as serviceberry, striped maple, leatherwood and witch hazel.

"Here, let me show you my gardening partner," said Jim as we made our way outside. Expecting someone to step out from behind a tree, I finally realized that he means nature. Nature is his gardening partner, and he's happy to follow her lead.

An Artist's Canvas

Toronto, Ontario

The Lounsburys' back garden in early spring is full of woodland beauties such as foamflower, with its white flower spikes. To the left of the flagstone path, groundcovers such as bloodroot, bellwort and mayapple flourish in the rich woodland soil.

Norma Lounsbury claims that her Toronto garden taught her to be ruthless when necessary, but I don't believe her. There's too much heart in this garden. But then again, there *is* evidence of incremental ruthlessness, and it's the non-natives that are the losers. If that counts as a heartless streak, then so be it.

Inclined to the step-by-step rather than the full-scale assault, Norma did a bit of nonnative shuffling before she relegated the exotics to the compost bin or to friends. (It's a shuffle I know well from my own garden. It's just too hard at first to do away with healthy exotics. But after a while, as the natives come into their own, the nonnatives begin to look out of place.)

Aside from her second-chance dance with nonnatives, hesitant is not a word that applies to Norma's efforts. When she began her native-plant woodland garden in Toronto about a decade ago, she dived right in. Using a method she'd read about, Norma put 10 layers of newspaper on top of the grass lawn, then soil on top of that. (She confesses that this was done under the cover of darkness, in a race against the clock.) Then she made holes in the grass-destroying mulch, and in went the native plants. "It works perfectly," says Norma. The grass gives up the ghost, weeds are smothered, the new plants are protected, and the resulting soil – when the newspaper breaks down – is rich and friable.

Norma has an artist's eye. As her husband, Bob, puts it, she treats her garden as an artist does a canvas. And though I've always found those designerly phrases beloved of landscape architects, such as harmony, balance, and so on, to be hopelessly vague and inherently inarticulable, Norma and Bob's garden proves that the language of description is ultimately beside the point – the coherence is all in the viewing, not the telling.

While the term *woodland garden* often conjures up images of deep green retreats, the northeastern woodland garden is, in fact, a colorful place in spring. In Bob and Norma Lounsbury's front-yard garden in Toronto, Ontario, perennials such as foamflower and trilliums burst into bloom.

Woodlands of the Northeastern Regions

WE'RE TRULY BLESSED in the Great Lakes, northeastern and mid-Atlantic regions with magnificent forests. The hardwood haven of maple, beech, oak, hickory and others has various labels (Deciduous Forest Region, for example) and much mythology. Stories of squirrels at the time of European contact being able to travel hundreds of miles without ever touching the ground, for instance, animate the imagination and give us our sense of living in a once forest-cloaked region.

How appropriate, then, that citizens across the region are engaged in enthusiastic tree-planting and reforestation efforts. Many gardeners, however, still get grumpy with all of this tree-talk, schooled as we are to mimic the sunny climes of the Mediterranean with our exotic plantings. Unfortunately, many gardeners still view shade as a problem to overcome, rather than a delightful opportunity. But the northeastern woodland garden is one of the true triumphs, one of the most appealing landscapes, the gardener can re-create.

A glowing carpet of Jacob's ladder provides spring color in the woodland garden.

First, though, a clarification about the term *woodland*. My dictionary defines it as "land covered with trees; forest." While some of us may be lucky enough to live on land covered with trees, many of us make do with one rangy street tree, which, in the spirit of urban compromise, I say counts as a forest – or, at the very least, as the beginning of a woodland garden. To my mind, so does a corner lot rendered deeply dim by surrounding tall buildings. Call it a woodland, and a woodland garden will follow, because in shade, the most sensible, appropriate garden to create is one that mimics a shady woodland.

Shade is a tricky term, though. The important thing is not the label but, rather, the degree and nature of your shade. Examine it thoroughly, get to know its quirks and oddities – its parts and partials and halves and deep and full. Learn its moods and modes, because shade is rarely uniform.

The street tree on my lot, for example – an exotic Norway maple that is both an exuberant shedder of mess *and* a vacuum cleaner of the arboreal world, soaking up all nutrients and moisture for miles – lets great swaths of morning light through to bathe the eastern side of the garden. This allows me some sun-loving woodland frauds: New England aster and black-eyed Susan. Such are the vagaries of the shade garden – immerse yourself in the details of your particular conditions. And, of course, exploit the oddities to the full in your design.

Woodland Wildflowers for the Northeastern Gardener

After making it through what is almost always a grueling and seemingly endless winter, northeastern gardeners truly earn the spring woodland show that is their due. Little compares with the explosive awakening that awaits in the woods in April and May, as the restorative smell of the Earth's litter richly exudes from each inch of ground.

Not only is the forest earth restorative to human senses, but it is indeed the forest's fuel and life-giver. Think of the work it takes to rake up the leaves from just one grand old tree in the front yard in fall; now multiply that leaf litter a hundredfold, and consider those dead leaves staying exactly where they fall. By the next summer, however, they'll be gone for the most part, returning all their goodness, nutrients and organic matter to the forest floor. Duff, it's called, and it's essential to the woods.

Think of the woodland garden, then, as a duffy place. Forget the neaten (and bleaken) fetish that so often characterizes our garden maintenance. Imagine a place richly renewed each year by the inevitable *stuff* that falls to the ground. Leave it be. Welcome it. Pile on more. Get some from neighbors. Give your woodland garden dead leaves, compost and leaf mulch. There's nothing like seeing the perky shoots of Solomon's seal poking a hole through a dead maple leaf in spring. Such force on a search for sun.

This drama unfolds each spring in the woodland garden. Before the tree canopy leafs out and sunlight becomes an endangered commodity, the spring plants grab every opportunity to bask in life-giving light. The great majority of them flower magnificently in spring, putting on a show that rivals any found in an exotic shade garden (indeed, the exotic-plant palette for shade color pales when compared with that of natives).

Some of these woodland plants – the spring ephemerals – put on their show and then go dormant under the ground, building up reserves of strength for next year's blast. But many others, after a long spring season of color, stay on with soothing greens and fascinating shapes and textures throughout the summer and fall. The native-plant woodland gardener is indeed blessed with an embarrassment of riches.

(Unless otherwise noted, all these woodland plants not only prefer but demand good, rich, humusy soil with average to moist conditions in shade.)

Red baneberry (*Actaea rubra*): Flowers are white but berries red, hence the name. Clusters of white flowers appear in early spring and look like slightly conical snowballs atop dark green foliage. It grows to about 2 feet (60 cm) and becomes quite bushy. Clusters of red berries are a knockout in summer.

Jack-in-the-pulpit (*Arisaema triphyllum*): A woodland *must* in moist, rich conditions, Jack-in-the-pulpit is a perky oddity: a spadix surrounded by a green hooded sheath. It grows 1 to 3 feet (30–90 cm) and produces orangish red berries in fall.

Wild ginger (*Asarum canadense*): The woodland gardener couldn't ask for an easier groundcover. Growing to about 6 inches (15 cm), wild ginger rapidly spreads its heart-shaped leaves to cover large areas. Though hidden by foliage, its maroon bell-shaped flowers in spring are worth a crouched peek.

The wildflower garden at Casa Loma in Toronto, Ontario, inspires with pleasing combinations and design ideas, such as Virginia bluebells (blue), wood poppy (yellow) and trillium (white).

THE WILD AND THE TAMED

TORONTO, ONTARIO

In a corner of Frank Kershaw's woodland, an old stump and a birdbath ensure that his garden will provide habitat for birds. Trilliums (white), wood poppies (yellow) and Virginia bluebells (blue) combine well with the white flowers of a saskatoon bush.

PURPOSEFUL PHRASES such as "perimeter belt" and "plant weavers" peppered Frank Kershaw's conversation as he showed me around his suburban Etobicoke garden, leading me to admit sheepishly that I know little of landscape-design lingo. But Frank was a gracious guide, and his long experience of giving gardening talks ensured that he could translate the language of design into the enthusiast's vernacular.

On his 55-by-150-foot (17 m x 46 m) property, Frank has amassed a collection of more than 375 species of plants, most of them natives, but he's quick to eschew what the numbers suggest: His is not some mini botanical garden – all disconnected display – but, rather, a carefully designed woodland planting of elegant proportions. Equal parts of Frank the horticulturist, Frank the gardener and Frank the native-plant promoter come into play in this garden, an evolving 14-year partnership between human inclinations and nature's imperatives.

The plant palette may be wild, but the resulting look is controlled and structured. Massed drifts of trilliums and wood poppies flow seamlessly into summer sweeps of wild geraniums and, later, culver's root, black snakeroot and asters. Spring's exuberant display leads to summer's calming greens and textures.

There are many secrets in this garden, many surprises, many rarities that demand exploration and reward with discovery. It's as if the pleasures of this garden are not announced but unfold on close observation – possibly even on one's hands and knees, peeking underneath or behind the blue cohosh and finding goldenseal or ginseng. Such crouched inspection is not, however, strictly necessary. There are plenty of broad statements made, and indeed, the garden was designed for viewing either from inside the house or from the family's lawn area, which surrounds the woodland.

It's somewhat unusual to find a controlled "wild" garden so tidily edged with lawn, but it's a logical juxtaposition that works, especially if you have kids who want the playful platform which lawns provide. What Frank has achieved is exactly that balance between chaos and control, fun and frame.

It is possible to create a woodland garden that mixes harmoniously with a more conventional landscape of grass lawn. In this suburban garden in Etobicoke, Ontario, Frank Kershaw has included a large section of lawn for family activities, and the woodland garden is designed around the perimeter of the property, where the surrounding trees provide a shady retreat.

This woodland was designed in drifts. Shimmering swaths of spring ephemerals, such as trilliums and Virginia bluebells, create an expansive effect, encouraging the eye to sweep across the bands of color.

After the first flush of spring exuberance, texture and foliage plants such as ferns create the dominant mood in the garden, and summer-blooming woodland plants such as black snakeroot provide color and interest.

Blue cohosh (*Caulophyllum thalictroides*): In the spring, this odd-looking and fascinating plant sends up dark bluish spiky shoots (which somewhat resemble peony shoots) that turn into bushy, rich green foliage. The flowers aren't dramatic (small and greenish yellow in spring), but the dark blue berries in fall are. It grows to about 2 1/2 feet (75 cm).

Goldenstar, a.k.a. green-and-gold (*Chrysogonum virginianum*): A dainty woodland groundcover (to 6 inches/15 cm), goldenstar produces loads of yellow daisylike flowers in spring through summer. Its dark green foliage provides an attractive contrast to the bright flowers.

Black snakeroot, a.k.a. bugbane (*Cimicifuga racemosa*): For wonky grace and summer flower, you can't beat black snakeroot. A large, bushy plant, it sends up a tall wand in midsummer that can reach as high as 5 feet (1.5 m) and is covered with white flowers. A stand of black snakeroot in the woodland garden, dappled with filtered light, is an arresting sight.

Dutchman's breeches (*Dicentra cucullaria*): With its nodding white flowers (with yellow tips) that hang down from arching stems in spring, Dutchman's breeches is a lovely plant which goes dormant in summer. Foliage is lacy and fernlike; grows to about 6 inches (15 cm).

Trout lily (*Erythronium americanum*): Another spring ephemeral, trout lily (sometimes called dog-tooth violet) is a low grower (6 inches/15 cm) with brownish spotted leaves and yellow bell-shaped nodding flowers. Best in carpeting masses.

The drooping yellow bells of bellwort combine well with the white trillium.

Wild strawberry (*Fragaria virginiana*): Another rapid spreader, wild strawberry is a great groundcover for open woodlands and woodland borders. (It does well in sunny meadows too.) Hugging the ground, it sends tendrils far and wide and, as a much-appreciated bonus, produces small flavor-packed berries. Flowers, which appear in spring and early summer, are white with yellow centers.

Wild geranium (*Geranium maculatum*): Not to be confused with the cultivated geranium (*Pelargonium*), the wild geranium is a woodland beauty. Purplish pink flowers cover the 1-to-2-foot-high (30–60 cm) plant from late spring to early summer, especially if deadheaded. Seedpods are also attractive, and their shape gives this plant its other common name: cranesbill.

Woodland sunflower (*Helianthus divaricatus*): In mid- to late summer, just when you're starting to think that color is over and done with in the woodland garden, the woodland sunflower kicks in with its bright yellow blossoms. Growing up to 5 feet (1.5 m) and creating dense colonies, this plant tolerates dry conditions.

Sharp-lobed hepatica (*Hepatica acutiloba*): Sharp-lobed hepatica is a small (to 6 inches/15 cm) but intriguing plant. Its delicate white or pink flowers appear in early spring, before the leaves, a harbinger of spring's regrowth. Leaves are three-lobed and often mottled with brown. Tolerates dry conditions.

Twinleaf (*Jeffersonia diphylla*): To my mind, this plant symbolizes everything great about many woodland plants: simple but stately. Its leaves are twin-lobed and a luminous green, its flowers white and starlike in spring. The seed capsule is pipe-shaped and hinged. It grows to about 1 foot (30 cm) in attractive clumps.

Canada lily (*Lilium canadense*): Near a woodland border, in open woodland conditions in moist soil, Canada lily makes a dramatic show. In midsummer, it sends up a tall stalk (to 5 feet/1.5 m) covered in orange, yellow or red blooms with out-curved petals.

Great lobelia, a.k.a. blue lobelia (*Lobelia siphilitica*): Easy to grow and striking for its tall (2 1/2 foot/75 cm) wands of blue flowers in mid- to late summer, great lobelia prefers moist conditions but will do well in regular soil in open shade.

Virginia bluebells (*Mertensia virginica*): I'm a sucker for blue, so this spring ephemeral is one of my favorites. Covered with blue (sometimes pinkish) trumpetlike nodding flowers in spring, this plant has pale, oval, smooth leaves. It grows to about 2 feet (60 cm) and positively glows when planted near wood poppy.

Bee balm, a.k.a. monarda (*Monarda didyma*): In light, open shade and moist conditions, you can't beat the entrancing red of bee balm's jester-hat-like flowers, which appear in midsummer and last for weeks. Great for hummingbirds, bees and butterflies, it grows to about 3 feet (1 m).

Wild blue phlox (*Phlox divaricata*): Growing to about 1 foot (30 cm), this groundcover dazzles with masses of blue flowers in spring. It spreads well and is easy to grow in moist to regular soil, full to part shade.

Mayapple (*Podophyllum peltatum*): Primarily of interest as a foliage plant (single white flowers are pretty but are hidden underneath the leaves in midspring), mayapple spreads to create dense colonies with huge umbrellalike leaves. It grows to about 1 1/2 feet (45 cm).

Jacob's ladder (*Polemonium reptans*): Masses of blue flowers in spring look fantastic when combined with trilliums or foamflower. It grows to about 1 foot (30 cm), spreads well and goes dormant in summer.

Solomon's seal (*Polygonatum biflorum*): If you have a problem area (say, under the drying shade of a Norway maple), Solomon's seal will quickly create a lush cover. It looks great throughout the seasons. In spring, its arching 3-foot (1 m) stems are covered with hanging white bell-shaped flowers; in summer, its bright green

A dazzling combination of creeping phlox (blue) and foamflower (white) at Longwood Gardens in Pennsylvania proves that a formal look can easily be achieved using native plants.

foliage glows; in fall, the leaves turn a soothing papery yellow, with blue-black berries hanging down.

Bloodroot (*Sanguinaria canadensis*): One of the earliest spring flowers, bloodroot sends up small, white starlike blooms, with leaves curled around the stalk. Watching the leaves unfurl into large saucers can easily become a welcome spring ritual. It grows about 6 to 10 inches (15–25 cm) and can get ratty during dry periods but is a very good woodland groundcover.

PLANTS FOR THE WOODLAND EDGE

Asters, black-eyed Susan, Canada anemone, goldenrod, jewelweed, wild columbine, wild geranium, woodland sunflower.

PLANTS FOR DRY SHADE

(two words that can strike fear in the woodland gardener's heart)

Canada mayflower, Canada violet, downy goldenrod, hay-scented fern, large-leaved aster, New York fern, white wood aster, wild onion.

Jim Hodgins' front-yard woodland in downtown Toronto, Ontario, contains more than 50 species native to the maple-beech forest ecosystem. Here, a yellow carpet of barren strawberry is surrounded with foamflower, wild ginger and prairie smoke (middle).

False Solomon's seal (*Smilacina racemosa*): Though the foliage of this plant, which grows 2¹/₂ feet (75 cm) high, resembles that of Solomon's seal, the flowers are quite different – clusters of creamy white at the end of arching stems. Bright red berries appear in summer; foliage turns gorgeous pale yellow in fall.

Blue-stemmed goldenrod (*Solidago caesia*): Although we think of goldenrod as a sunny-meadow and prairie plant, a number of species do well in shade. Blue-stemmed goldenrod, for example, is particularly good in dry shady conditions, with its blue-green cast and yellow flowers in late summer. It grows 1 to 3 feet (30–90 cm) and is not aggressive. Use it at the woodland edge.

Wood poppy, a.k.a. celandine poppy (*Stylophorum diphyllum*): I wasn't much of a yellow fan until I got to know this merry and prolific woodlander. Covered with yellow blooms in spring, the wood poppy grows to about 1¹/₂ feet (45 cm) in large clumps. Breathtaking when combined with Virginia bluebells and trilliums. (Be careful not to confuse it with the nonnative invasive celandine, *Chelidonium majus*.)

Meadowrue (*Thalictrum dioicum*): Early meadowrue is a delightful problem solver in dry open-shade conditions. Its foliage resembles that of columbine (I made the mistake of planting them together, so unfortunately, neither one shows to good effect), and its flowers are small, whitish green and drooping in midspring. It grows to about 2¹/₂ feet (75 cm).

Foamflower (*Tiarella cordifolia*): Masses of foamflower, with spikes of white starlike blossoms in spring, make a stunning sight, especially when combined with Virginia bluebells and wild blue phlox. Good as a groundcover in heavy to light shade, foamflower grows to about 1 foot (30 cm) and spreads well.

Winning Combos

- barren strawberry, pasqueflower
- bloodroot, twinleaf, wood poppy
- sessile trillium, tall meadowrue, wild blue phlox, wood poppy
- false rue anemone, trillium
- bloodroot, blue cohosh, false Solomon's seal, sharp-lobed hepatica

The native wild geranium provides a welcome purplish blue in the woodland garden. Not to be confused with the exotic geranium (*Pelargonium*), the native geranium combines well with foamflower.

White trillium (*Trillium grandiflorum*): A signature plant of the woodland garden, white trillium is prized for its gorgeous white flowers, which become pinkish as they mature. Lasting throughout spring, the trillium goes dormant in summer. It grows to about 1 foot (30 cm).

Large-flowered bellwort, a.k.a. great merrybells (*Uvularia grandiflora*): Of all the plants in my front woodland garden, this one most often elicits comments – people are drawn to the drooping pale yellow bells in spring. Growing to about 2 feet (60 cm), it looks stunning with Virginia bluebells.

Canada violet (*Viola canadensis*): There are many violets from which the woodland gardener can choose, but Canada violet remains one of the most readily available in the nursery trade and one of the finest. White flowers with purplish veins and yellow centers appear in early spring. It grows to about 8 inches (20 cm) and looks best in masses.

Barren strawberry (*Waldsteinia fragarioides*): A low-growing groundcover (to 10 inches/25 cm), barren strawberry is a garden-saver in dry woodland conditions. It covers the earth quickly and, in spring, produces masses of small yellow flowers. Its foliage, dark green and glossy, looks wonderful throughout the summer and sets off other plants well.

For a splash of summer woodland color, try midsummer bloomers such as Michigan lily and bee balm, both of which prefer moist conditions.

CARPETS UNDER CANOPIES

Trees are the defining feature of the woodland garden, but they can also create problem conditions when their feeder roots, always on a hunt for moisture and nutrients, grab water and nutrients from other plants, making it difficult to grow anything underneath the canopy. (The nonnative Norway maple is especially notorious in this regard. I've collected over a dozen quotes from gardening books and magazines which categorically state that it's impossible to grow anything under Norway maples – a statement that gardeners throughout the region have managed to defy.)

Luckily, there are some good native woodlanders for the base of trees. Wild ginger, for example, will flourish and grow into dense colonies. Ferns, with their shallow, wiry roots, do well under trees, particularly those species adapted to drier woodland conditions, such as hay-scented fern. Groundcovers such as bloodroot or foamflower can also be used around the base of trees, creating a low-maintenance carpet of green. And for highly acid beds, such as those under conifers, try Canada mayflower or partridgeberry.

A Woodland Slope

Pittsburgh, Pennsylvania

Esther Allen's ingenious and effective deer fence makes use of fallen branches to fill in the holes that deer left in the chicken wire.

Esther Allen has a theory that should cheer the heart of any messy house-keeper: "I find that people are either good housekeepers or good gardeners." I didn't peek inside Esther's house, but I suspect that she's as careful inside as she is outside; it may just be that she's expanded the notion of housekeeping to include making a home for birds and other creatures out-of-doors as well.

Esther's landscape was alive with birds as she showed us her woodland wonder. Twelve to eighteen species visit every day; in the winter, wild turkeys parade. But while she welcomes the birds, other creatures, such as raccoons and deer, are an ongoing problem.

She's tried the hanging-soap trick; the deer ate it. She's tried a wire fence; the deer just jumped right over that. But gradually, as the deer poked holes in the chicken wire, she filled them in with woven branches, creating an attractive fence that, while not 100 percent deerproof, is at least a deterrent and is a perfect backdrop to the woodland vista.

Perhaps the most appropriate tool in Esther's kit of tricks is her philosophy: "I pretty much let things take care of themselves." Her approach extends to everything from compost ("I just leave things where they fall") to seedlings ("I tend to let stuff grow wherever it comes up") to paths ("I make them wherever I want to wander") to dead trees, which she leaves as snags for wildlife.

Esther's accommodating approach (she prefers to call it "lazy") has rewarded her well. Starting 30 years ago with a bare plot, just one spruce tree and bad soil, she gradually enriched her property with dead leaves and compost, building the proper woodland conditions from the ground up. She planted trees, dozens of them – black alder, black walnut, buckeye, cucumber-tree, fringetree, Kentucky coffee tree, maple, redbud, serviceberry and more, many started from seed. And shrubs – maple-leaved viburnum, spicebush, witch hazel. And native wildflowers, rescued from development sites and raised from seed.

She started with plants that are easy to grow, such as blue-eyed Mary, goldenseal, Jacob's ladder and Virginia waterleaf; then, as the soil improved, she added more difficult woodlanders, the orchids and trilliums and aniseroot that demand good soil. As Esther drifted into more demanding experiments, the woodland plants moved farther down the slope; she started wildflowers at the back of the property, at the top of the hill, then moved them forward as the shade developed and the woodland plants filled in the shady spots.

While we wandered, Esther picked up seeds and tossed them here and there, proving her point about the garden's structure: "This just evolved." And with evolution come surprises: "I keep finding things I didn't know I had." Forty-five species of trees and more than one hundred species of wildflowers later, Esther's advice – "just let them do their own thing" – seems less like laziness and more like very good housekeeping.

Esther Allen's woodland garden in Pittsburgh, Pennsylvania, is based not on rigid design but on a fortuitous and forgiving philosophy of random chance: "This isn't a structured garden. This just evolved." Here, a yellow lady's slipper (middle) is surrounded by bloodroot and trilliums.

FERNS FOR THE WOODLAND GARDENER

Despite the relative ease with which many native ferns grow, I must confess that they remain somewhat of a mystery to me. I've had just too many frustrating fern failures to get cocky and blasé about growing them. Instead, I consider every fern success a gift and every dead fern a personal challenge from the foliage deity to do it right next time. (Unfortunately, I have more than a few crispy fronds on my conscience.)

The reason I continue to soldier on, adding new native ferns every season, is that native ferns are essential in the woodland garden. They're also the perfect indicator plant – the botanical equivalent of the canary in the coal mine. When the ferns are happy, I know that I have finally achieved that long-sought-after and absolutely necessary humusy, friable, nutrient-rich woodland soil. Anything less, and no wonder these forest denizens say *sayonara*.

Although I've mouthed my fair share of fern propaganda over the years based on the idea that they're wonderful as filler, hiding the holes left by more desirable ephemerals, I've decided that this is a disservice to ferns. In their own right, ferns can dazzle and mesmerize, if treated with respect – that is, if treated as individuals, with all their diversity embraced.

The unfurling fronds of the ostrich fern.

(Unless otherwise noted, the ferns listed here all require good, rich, well-drained humusy soil and regular to moist conditions. If you've got clay or sandy soil, add lots of compost to the fern bed. When planting ferns, position the crown at the soil's surface, not below ground.)

Maidenhair fern (*Adiantum pedatum*): With its purplish black forked stems, from which fronds radiate in semi-circles, the maidenhair exudes elegance – a woodland must. Keep it moist and protected from strong winds, and don't disturb its shallow roots by cultivating too close to the plant (good advice for *any* fern). It grows 1 to 3 feet (30–90 cm).

Lady fern (*Athyrium filix-femina*): With its lacy leaves, the lady fern is perfect for the woodland edge because it tolerates some sun as long as the soil is moist, although it also does well in full shade. It grows 1 to 3 feet (30–90 cm) and spreads well.

Hay-scented fern (*Dennstaedtia punctilobula*): At the woodland edge, hay-scented fern is a good choice if you want a quick cover. Growing to about 1½ feet (45 cm), it exudes a sweet scent when its fronds are bruised or cut. Tolerates dryish soil.

Male fern (*Dryopteris filix-mas*): A dramatic fern with dark green fronds, the male fern grows 2 to 3 feet (60–90 cm). Sun to shade; moist soil.

Oak fern (*Gymnocarpium dryopteris*): If you're looking for a low-growing fern as a groundcover for deep shade, oak fern is it. Its triangular three-part fronds seem to float in lacy mats parallel to the ground. It grows to about 10 inches (25 cm).

Ostrich fern (*Matteuccia pensylvanica*): Versatile and easy to grow, the ostrich fern will spread wantonly in most conditions. Its light green fronds brighten the garden, and its tasty fiddleheads enliven the spring dinner table. It grows to about 3 feet (1 m). Sun to full shade; moist soil.

Sensitive fern (*Onoclea sensibilis*): A good choice for moist semi-shaded sites, the sensitive fern reaches 2½ feet

(75 cm) and is therefore best for large gardens, especially since it spreads rapidly. Its fronds are scalloped and light green. Semi-shade; moist soil.

Cinnamon fern (*Osmunda cinnamomea*): A versatile fern for sun or shade, cinnamon fern needs moisture and acidic soil. Its size (3–4 feet/90–120 cm) makes a grand statement, but also very appealing are its white, woolly fiddleheads in spring, which look a bit like well-fed plushy caterpillars all curled up for protection.

Interrupted fern (*Osmunda claytoniana*): Looking similar to the cinnamon fern but not as tall (to 2 1/2 feet/ 75 cm), interrupted fern prefers moist open-woodland conditions.

Rock fern (*Polypodium virginianum*): The evergreen rock fern is great in rock gardens, which mimic its native habitat of cliff and crevice. A relatively compact fern (growing to about 1 foot/30 cm) with leathery leaves, it requires good drainage. Partial to full shade; drought-tolerant.

Christmas fern (*Polystichum acrostichoides*): An evergreen clump-forming fern with leathery leaves, Christmas fern looks dazzling against the snow, with its deep green, glossy leaves. It grows to about 2 1/2 feet (75 cm). Light to deep shade; tolerates dryish soil.

New York fern (*Thelypteris noveboracensis*): The delicate leaves of the New York fern turn a wonderful yellow in fall. A quick grower, this fern has narrow, tapering fronds of luminous green and grows 2 feet (60 cm) in filtered shade.

In the woodland garden, dense plantings of ferns, such as the cinnamon ferns here, create a cool oasis. The colorful blooms of trilliums and Virginia bluebells punctuate the display in spring. The shrub (upper left) is leatherwood.

WINNING COMBOS

- foamflower, New York fern, wood poppy
- broad beech fern, white baneberry, wood poppy
- Goldie's fern, maidenhair fern
- Christmas fern, mayapple
- oak fern, yellow trillium
- bloodroot, Jack-in-the-pulpit, wild ginger, wood fern
- starflower, wood fern

Lush ferns enhance the calming effect of a pond.

The Magic of Moss

On a bed of moss, delightfully charming bluets create an attractive and no-maintenance alternative to lawn grass in Dave Benner's garden.

Reflecting on the recent interest in native-plant gardening, Dave Benner says, "It's about time." He's been doing it since 1962, and it must be gratifying to him to see the idea catch on.

Dave comes to native-plant gardening from a very practical position. He wanted a beautiful garden at his New Hope, Pennsylvania, home – but with no maintenance. "That's my whole philosophy: no weeding, no watering." He now boasts that he hasn't weeded in 10 years: the evergreen groundcovers are so thick, there's no bare soil in which weeds can take hold.

And what groundcovers they are – over 40 different species, including masses of shortia, probably the largest stand of this rare gem in any private garden in the Northeast. After I tell him of my problems getting bottle gentians started from seed, he tantalizes me with tales of just scattering seeds and watching them pop up like weeds. The secret of propagation, he says, is moss – "the best propagation medium there is." The way he arrived at his spongy cushioning carpet is another story of no-work gardening.

Three weeks after moving in and realizing that he had no intention of mowing two acres (0.8 ha) of grass, Dave simply sprinkled sulfur dust and ammonium sulfate and watched the grass die. Six weeks later, he raked up the grass, exposing the poor acidic clay soil. After that, the moss, already out back with the oaks, moved in – 25 to 30 different kinds of it, none of which he planted. Instead, he created the conditions that moss enjoys, and let nature do the work. (Dave points out, though, that he is lucky to live in a small town, since moss is sensitive to air pollution and will not survive in polluted environments.) "In two years, the property went from grass lawns to moss 'lawns' without my doing anything." Words for the low-maintenance gardener to live by.

Dave Benner's woodland garden in New Hope, Pennsylvania, is both stunning and low maintenance. The native groundcovers of foamflower, trillium, wild blue phlox and wood poppy are so thick, no weeds can take hold. As a result, Dave hasn't had to weed in more than 10 years.

Weeds and Woodlands

My suspicion is that while many gardeners complain about weeding, most of us secretly enjoy the activity. After all, it's a chance to commune hand-to-dirt with the garden and to investigate at ground level what's hidden beneath showier tall plants. Weeding provides the gardener with a purpose, a task to remind us that we're still needed.

Woodland gardens, though, truly are ideal for the weed-hating gardener, since so many of our common North American weed plants, such as dandelion and burdock, are sun-lovers. Once the woodland garden is carpeted with groundcovering species, which provide a kind of protective shield, weeds will rarely be a problem. Chances are good that woodland gardeners will have more trouble keeping exuberant natives such as Canada anemone and Virginia waterleaf under control than keeping out weedy invaders.

However, there are a few weedy, even invasive, non-natives that can cause problems in woodland gardens (and, worse, in wild areas). Garlic mustard, for example, is a common invader. In many woodlands, it has taken over the understory, crowding out diverse communities of natives, and it will easily behave the same way in gardens if action isn't taken on first sighting. Common buckthorn is a shrub or small tree that can also crowd out natives in the woodland and so should be controlled.

Spreading groundcovers such as Virginia waterleaf (front middle), Virginia bluebells (blue), mayapple (back middle) and wood poppy (yellow) ensure that weeds cannot gain a foothold in the woodland garden.

An ongoing problem for native-plant gardeners, particularly those outside major urban centers, is the availability of native plants in the nursery trade. Although more and more nurseries now carry native wildflowers, shrubs and trees, these plants are still not as readily available as exotics. As well, some native plants carried by the nursery trade are grown from parent stock that originates a great distance away from where the plant will eventually find a home. Thus, although the plant is technically a "native," it may not be adapted to local conditions.

To deal with this problem and to encourage the propagation of genetically appropriate indigenous plants, some small nurseries (many of them community-based projects) are springing up throughout North America. One such nursery is the MacPhail Woods Ecological Forestry Project in Orwell, Prince Edward Island, which collects local tree seeds and propagates them for sale to gardeners. The path to the nursery gate leads visitors through an inspiring demonstration garden.

Of Bogs and Bathtubs

Saginaw, Michigan

"Prolific" is the word for the Cases' propagation successes.

"They say it's not growable, but that's not true. It's perfectly growable." This comment comes up over and over in Fred and Roberta Case's garden in Michigan. Pick a fussy plant, and chances are, the Cases not only have grown it but have watched it turn into something of a pest. A relative pest, for it's hard to imagine ever attaching that label to lewisias, orchids and pitcher plants.

Most gardeners would give anything for the Cases' lovely pests: 3-foot-tall (90 cm) Jack-in-the-pulpits, mayapples ("like the Medusa – chop off one head, and six more come up," says Fred), the airy black snakeroot filling the woods, where 38 species of trilliums have, throughout the years, flourished....

Along with the Cases' woodland expertise and trillium show, it's the six-year-old bog garden that has made their garden famous. "What most people mean by a bog garden is a wet spot of very easy-to-grow water plants," says Fred. Not their bog, which is the real thing: a highly acidic peat-rich watery enclave in which pitcher plants, pogonias, white fringed orchids, even the Venus flytrap, make their home (except in summer, when some of the pitcher plants move to their vacation home – a bathtub bed used for propagation).

The practical knowledge gleaned from hands-on growing is clearly what animates the Cases' experiments. "We know we're crazy," says Fred, "but we have fun being crazy." Witness Roberta on a steamy summer afternoon, in her bathing suit and to her knees *in* the bog, weeding or pulling out leaves. Or, in a normal year, the 500 native plants all started from seed. (One is afraid to ask what happens in an overzealous year.) "But if you don't grow it," says Roberta, "you lose that knowledge. There's so much to learn by growing."

In other words, don't trust the experts or the books that say "impossible." Give that fussy plant a try, and you, too, may discover, as the Cases did, the rose pogonia that will reward you with 225 flowers three years from now. The trick? "Many of the so-called hard plants are not really that hard. It's simply a matter of getting the seedlings established." Whether in a bathtub or an expensive greenhouse, you just need to get your hands dirty.

Pitcher plants in Fred and Roberta Case's Saginaw, Michigan, bog garden.

Black-eyed Susan (foreground), New England aster (middle left), thin-leaved coneflower (back right), sneezeweed (top right-hand corner) and calico aster (white, right) create a wonderful show in late summer and provide nectar and seed sources for butterflies, moths and birds.

SUNNY MEADOWS IN THE NORTHEASTERN REGIONS

ALTHOUGH THE DECIDUOUS forest is the defining feature of the region, it often surprises people to hear that southwestern Ontario is within the most easterly range of the tallgrass prairie ecosystem (though there are, in fact, a few rare prairie communities in northern Ontario). As well, prior to settlement, many disturbance factors, such as fire and windstorms, led to gaps in forest cover and thus open clearings of sun-loving plant communities in the northeastern regions. For the gardener whose lot is treeless and who, for whatever reason, has no plans to plant trees, this sunny-meadow model can form the basis of a native-plant garden.

There is a bit of debate within native-plant circles about the true nature of meadows in the northeastern regions. Some purists point to the fact that because meadows are transitional communities (i.e., nature's stopgap healing measure as the forest returns after some kind of disturbance), they are not stable climax ecosystems which perpetuate themselves. The implication is that it makes little sense to impede nature's progressive march to forest by maintaining a meadow in a permanent meadow state. True enough, but irrelevant to the native-plant gardener who favors sun-loving meadow forbs and wants to maintain a meadow-plant community over time. No permit or permission required.

To my mind, the appeal of meadow-plant communities, particularly in the urban environment, is that they stand as an acknowledgment that a disturbance has occurred. The meadow is an attempt to absorb that disturbance into nature's model and turn it to advantage. For the meadow is truly a healing place: It's where nature tries to heal disturbed land, setting in motion the process of succession to stable climax communities. The meadow gardener simply telescopes a 150-year process (the average length of time it takes for the climax forest to return) into a moment that appeals to his or her garden aesthetic: compromise turned as "natural" as climax.

Another reason the meadow model is so appropriate in urban situations is that native meadow forbs tend to be very easy to grow, creating showy gardens in next to no time. You can plant seedlings of so many beautiful wildflowers in spring and expect to have blooms that first summer. Usually by the next year, and certainly by the third year, the meadow will look mature and lived in, all with very little work (other than vigilant weeding, that is).

And, best of all, again for urban situations especially, is the fact that meadow communities thrive in conditions that would otherwise sound like write-offs: poor soil, unimproved by masses of organic material; periods of drought; sandy or gravelly soil; and so on. Meadow plants will, for the most part, feel right at home under such degraded conditions (unless otherwise noted in the following list). No need for the gardener to fuss and toil at improvements.

Golden ragwort is a plant of sunny, moist meadows, though it will also grow in part shade. Here, it combines well with wild blue phlox, which also blooms in late spring.

Blue star can be used as a bushy foliage plant, but its prolific blue flowers are also charming in late spring.

MEADOW WILDFLOWERS FOR THE NORTHEASTERN GARDENER

Blue star, a.k.a. blue dogbane (*Amsonia tabernaemontana*): Though its flowers are nice (blue and appearing in late spring), blue star is also good as an erect, bushy foliage plant. It grows to 3 feet (90 cm). Sun to part shade; prefers moist conditions but will do just fine in regular soil.

Smooth aster (*Aster laevis*): There are so many native asters from which to choose, all of them adaptable and forgiving. Smooth aster produces masses of bluish lavender flowers (with yellow centers) in fall and grows to about 3 feet (90 cm). Sun; moist to dry soil.

Boltonia (*Boltonia asteroides*): My boltonia is a flopper that has never done particularly well, but that's probably because it's in a spot which is too shady (and slightly outside its native range). It grows tall (4–6 feet/1.2–2 m) and produces masses of white asterlike flowers in late summer, lasting through fall. Sun; dry to moist soil.

Wild senna (*Cassia hebecarpa*): Wild senna looks like a shrub because of its tall (to 6 feet/2 m), bushy nature. Leaves are delicate, though, almost feathery, and its yellow pealike flowers appear in late summer. Full to part sun; drought-tolerant; sandy soil, though also does well in moist sites.

Turtlehead (*Chelone glabra*): At the woodland edge, in part sun, white turtlehead will flourish if the site is moist enough. In profile, the flowers do look like turtleheads, sort of wonky and curious, as if they're sticking their necks out to investigate. Turtlehead grows 3 to 5 feet (1–1.5 m) and is good for attracting butterflies. Part to full sun; moist soil.

Coreopsis (*Coreopsis lanceolata*): Gold-yellow daisylike flowers appear in midsummer and are long-lasting, particularly if deadheaded. Growing to about 1½ feet (45 cm) and spreading well, it also attracts butterflies. Sun; dry to average soil; drought-tolerant.

Showy tick-trefoil (*Desmodium canadense*): I'm pretty sure that the seeds often attached to my cat's fur in early fall are the "ticks" of showy tick-trefoil, which attests to the perambulating, spreading nature of this easy-to-grow

Bluets and wild strawberry have a tenacious ability to proliferate even in the tiniest hold.

native legume (and to the perambulating, spreading nature of my feline). Dense spikes of pink to lavender flowers cluster at the top of this tall grower (4–6 feet/ 1.2–2 m) in summer. It produces dense stands rather quickly and is great larval food for butterflies. Sun; average soil.

Fireweed (*Epilobium angustifolium*): Perhaps all native plants with "weed" in their names should be retitled, but fireweed does have a tendency to take over (and calling it willow herb won't disguise the fact). Spikes of bright magenta blooms cover the plant in summer; leaves are narrow, stems reddish. Plumes of feathery seedpods in late summer give the plant a delicate, airy appearance. Grows 5 to 6 feet (1.5–2 m). Sun; regular soil.

Bottle gentian, a.k.a. closed gentian (*Gentiana andrewsii*): Bottle gentian easily has the most striking blue flowers of any plant I know. It positively glows. What's more, the flowers are a fascinating shape: closed and rounded oblong, in clusters at the top of the plant in late summer. It grows 1 to 2 feet (30–60 cm), with glossy leaves. Full sun to part shade; moist soil.

Sunflower (*Helianthus annuus*): An annual, sunflower has a rough, hairy stem and heart-shaped leaves and produces brown-centered yellow flowers that bloom from midsummer through autumn. It grows 3 to 10 feet (1–3 m) and is a dramatic addition to the meadow garden. Easy to grow. Adaptable in terms of soil, from moist to dry, but needs full sun.

Swamp rose-mallow (*Hibiscus moscheutos* subsp. palustris, a.k.a. *H. palustris*): I can't think of a native perennial

A rampant spreader, fireweed looks best when grown in showy masses.

For late-summer color, you can't beat obedient plant, one of the easiest natives to grow – and the competition for easiest-to-grow title is stiff! Obedient plant is also a source of nectar for butterflies.

flower in the northeastern regions that's larger than that of the swamp rose-mallow – its round, pinkish flowers look almost tropical. Growing to about 6 feet (2 m), it flowers in midsummer and often continues to bloom until early fall. Sun; moist soil.

Bluets (*Houstonia caerulea*): Creating a stunning carpet of blue, violet or white, bluets are tiny, delicate flowers that appear in spring through midsummer. Grassy foliage is low-growing, barely rising from the ground to about 3 inches (7.6 cm). It is particularly attractive when grown in moss. Sun to filtered light.

Jewelweed (*Impatiens capensis*): At the meadow's woodland edge, the annual jewelweed provides a blast of orange from mid- to late summer. Growing tall (up to 5 feet/1.5 m) and creating large stands, jewelweed produces tubular flowers that are loved by hummingbirds, bees and butterflies. It self-sows year after year. Sun to part shade; moist soil.

For spring color in the sunny to part-shade garden, try shooting star.

Turk's-cap lily (*Lilium superbum*): Turk's-cap lily is dramatic and gorgeous. Its orange blooms are spotted with maroonish brown and appear in midsummer. It grows tall (5–6 feet/1.5–2 m) and needs good drainage. Flower petals recurve, hence the name. Sun to part sun; moist soil.

Cardinal flower (*Lobelia cardinalis*): Nothing beats the cardinal flower's striking tubular red flower spikes in mid- to late summer. It grows 2 to 4 feet (60–120 cm) and attracts hummingbirds and butterflies. There's a mulch debate about this one, and since I've killed two cardinal flowers – one mulched, one not – I've followed the debate with great interest. I'm with Carol Ottesen, who, in her book *The Native Plant Primer*, suggests that cardinal flower should be mulched over the winter but warns that the mulch should be removed in spring; otherwise, the plant will rot. Sun to part shade; moist soil.

Beardtongue, a.k.a. foxglove penstemon (*Penstemon digitalis*): White tubular flowers appear in early summer and last for weeks. Foliage consists of low-growing rosettes, from which tall flower stalks (2–4 feet/60–120 cm) with glossy leaves emerge. Beardtongue attracts hummingbirds. Sun to part shade; dry to moist soil.

Phlox (*Phlox paniculata*): Snowball flowers in pink clusters make phlox an attractive garden plant in mid- to late summer. Unfortunately, it often suffers from powdery mildew, especially if the plant is crowded and air circulation is poor, but this doesn't kill it. Phlox grows tall (from 3–6 feet/1–2 m). Sun to part shade; average soil.

Obedient plant (*Physostegia virginiana*): Also known as false dragonhead (though I've yet to encounter a true dragonhead), obedient plant produces wonderful spikes covered in pinkish snapdragonlike flowers in late summer through fall. Growing to about 3 feet (1 m), obedient plant isn't the least bit fussy; indeed, some people find it invasive. Sun; average to moist soil.

Spiderwort (*Tradescantia virginiana*): Spiderwort proves a rapid grower. Its blue-purple flowers appear in late spring and are long-lasting. Leaves are irislike and tend to flop over by midsummer. It grows 1 to 2 feet (30–60 cm) and can be invasive. Part shade to sun; tolerates dry, sandy soil as well as moist sites.

GRASSES FOR NATIVE MEADOWS

I must admit that I'm a little put off by the term "ornamental grasses," since *all* native grasses have ornamental potential. And they all have functional potential too – as structural support for tall-growing wildflowers, as deep-rooted soil builders and as seed sources for birds.

While nature's meadows are splashy, colorful places full of blooming wildflowers, they are also grassy places, often with a high proportion of grasses to wildflowers. Why not broaden the garden's ornamental palette to include the swaying subtle pleasures that grasses provide?

Grasses to try: June grass, little bluestem, northern dropseed, sideoats grama, switchgrass.

"Native-plant and wildlife gardening go together," says Fred Oehmichen of his and his partner Sandra Barone's garden in rural Quebec, near the town of Oka. On a 10-acre (4 ha) site with spectacular views of forested hills and a lake (the *second* best view around, says Fred; the Oka Monastery has the best view), their garden was built to attract wildlife – in particular, birds, butterflies and small animals.

Fred and Sandra's training in landscape design is obvious, as they point out delightful combinations such as a corner with serviceberry, cedar, birch and sumac, which promises a blaze of glorious fall color.

Water-efficient principles have been incorporated into the garden. The pond, for instance, is fed by a downspout from the roof. Frogs were in full frolic on the day I visited, and the native water lily in full bloom.

Attracting Wildlife to the Garden

This garden mixture of natives and non-natives was designed by Victor Chanasyk of Guelph, Ontario, with butterfly attraction in mind. Natives include red bee balm, orange butterfly weed and the drying spikes of blazing star.

I'VE MET SO MANY deer-plagued gardeners (and seen a lot of Solomon's plume missing their plumes) that the idea of going out of one's way to *attract* wildlife to the garden starts to sound like heresy – either that or a realistic warning that you may have some unexpected results once you begin to garden for wildlife. Indeed, it's a good idea to question your reasons for wanting to attract wildlife in the first place. It *sounds* very appealing, but are you truly willing to share your garden home with other creatures – *all* other creatures – or do you want to pick and choose the species that find food and refuge in your garden?

These may sound like crass questions (picking and choosing as if at a supermarket!), but it's better to confront your biases in advance than to confront a nibbling deer with anger, frustration and a newfound enthusiasm for artillery. Instead of starry-eyed ideas about nature's benign munificence, think food chain. Think occasional territorial skirmish. Think snapped Solomon's seals and targeted twinflowers.

And, yes, think life. If you're willing to participate in the necessary give and take of gardening for wildlife, the rewards are rich. Your garden will become not just a place of ornamental beauty but a healthy habitat, home and haven for creatures that are losing too much of it in the wild.

Whether it's birds, butterflies, bees, moths, toads, frogs, opossums, bats, shrews – or all of them – the key to attracting critters to the garden is to create the conditions that meet their food, water and cover requirements. Not to anthropomorphize, but think of the basic things that humans need in order to feel comfortably at home. Other animals need pretty much the same things (minus the video machine and bookshelves). In other words, you must provide the basic necessities of life in the habitat garden. Of course, it's made more complicated by the fact that different species have different specific requirements, but the broad categories of food, water and cover apply in general to all.

The good news is that if you're already committed to the idea of using native plants, you're well on the way to creating a wildlife-friendly habitat garden. Indigenous wildlife and native flora have evolved together over thousands of years, coexisting and meeting the others' needs in fascinating (and sometimes surprising) ways. For instance, the hummingbird's bill is perfectly adapted to extract nectar from flowers; some wildflower species wrap their seeds in "ant snacks" so that ants will carry them away and plant them elsewhere; the "bull's-eye" pattern on some flowers can be seen only by moths and guides them to land and pick up pollen to deposit on other plants, hence assisting in reproduction. Once you're aware of such interactions between plants and wildlife, a whole other dimension to the garden unfolds.

Berries, such as the fruit of red baneberry, provide an important food source for wildlife.

Plants with Deerproof Potential: bittersweet, blue-eyed grass, Jack-in-the-pulpit, mayapple (lower photo), nodding onion, red trillium, trumpet vine, Virginia creeper, wild ginger, wild leek (top photo).

The following are some general points to consider in your efforts to create creature comforts. (For a more detailed list of plant species that will attract wildlife, see the plants listed in this chapter or refer to any of the books mentioned in the Sources section at the end of the book.)

Food: In the garden, one of the primary food sources will be the plants. Some creatures, such as butterflies in their larval stage, feed on foliage. Others, among them butterflies in their adult stage, hummingbirds, moths and bees, feed on flower nectar. Still others, such as birds, feed on seeds, nuts and berries. If you plant natives, you will attract these creatures.

Another fabulous food source in the garden is insect life. Again, if you plant natives, chances are that you'll also have a rich diversity of insects in the garden, and these become dinner, lunch, breakfast and snacks for all kinds of creatures, from birds to bats.

Though most North Americans tend to be squeamish about bugs (how else to explain the roaring trade in insecticides, when by far the vast majority of insects are beneficial to the garden?), the native-plant gardener instead sees bugs as beneficial pollinators, useful predators (lacewings eating the aphids, for example) and delectable food fodder for the other creatures they attract. Retire the chemical poisons, and watch the feast begin.

Along with plants and insects, other options for providing wildlife food include bird feeders, suet balls, etc., for birds. Because different styles of feeders and different foods attract different bird species, consult a good bird-feeding book (listed in the Sources section) before putting up feeders.

Well, it's my turn to admit to some starry-eyed indulgence in the above, for there's no doubt that some creatures – deer immediately come to mind – can wreak havoc with their food forays in the garden. Try the tricks – hang soap on a rope, or place human hair in mini hairdressing-salon piles around the garden – but if all else fails, you'll need to resort to a fence, a *high* fence (7–8 feet/ 2–2.5 m). I'm quite partial to a black-mesh deer fence developed and sold by Dave Benner in Pennsylvania – it is almost invisible from 20 feet (6 m) away and is easy to install (contact Benner's Gardens, 6974 Upper York Road, New Hope, Pennsylvania 18938).

Cover: All creatures need some kind of cover or shelter at various stages of their life cycles and at different times of the day. As well, different species have different requirements in terms of the amount of space they need.

Some require ground-level shelter; others require shelter at different heights. Most gardeners naturally provide a diversity of layers in the garden by planting groundcovers, herbaceous wildflowers, shrubs and trees.

It helps, as well, to resist the impulse to tidy everything. Fallen branches and dead stumps, for instance, turn into their own mini ecosystems, supporting all kinds of wildlife. If you've got the space, brush piles – far from being an eyesore – become rich habitat for birds and mammals.

If you're thinking of adding birdhouses to the garden, refer to the books listed in the Sources section at the end of the book, as it's important to build or buy a birdhouse that is appropriate and safe. (Some designs are notoriously easy for nest predators to invade.)

One of my favorite forms of cover, and something on the cutting edge of gardening, relates to rock piles, or hibernacula, for snakes. Perhaps if more of us had experience with these nonthreatening (for the most part) creatures, snakes would shed their dangerous connotations. Sunny rock piles, where the harmless garter snake, for example, can slither and squirm (and get hungry for slugs), might start the process of demystifying the class Reptilia, suborder Serpentes.

Water: A major water feature, such as a pond, appeals to humans and to wildlife, but a water feature for wildlife can also take less dramatic forms. A birdbath, for example, provides a drinking and cleaning source for birds, but you must keep it clean, and you shouldn't place it too close to predators' perches (such as shrubs). A simple bowl or some other arrangement to hold standing water will also work, though it will be a perfect breeding ground for mosquitoes.

For those gardeners interested in frogs and toads, you can't do better than to build a pond.

Hummingbirds love the stunning red cardinal flower.

Both the Canadian Wildlife Federation and the National Wildlife Federation have produced plenty of information for homeowners interested in landscaping for wildlife. (The National Wildlife Federation also certifies backyards as wildlife-friendly habitat.) Contact the National Wildlife Federation's Backyard Habitat Program, 1400–16th Street NW, Washington, D.C. 20036-2266, Web site: ‹http://www.nwf.org/nwf/habitats/›. Or contact the Canadian Wildlife Federation's Habitat 2000 Program, 2740 Queensview Drive, Ottawa, Ontario K2B 1A2, Web site: ‹http://www.cwf-fcf.org›.

Shrubs for the Northeastern Gardener

꙼

Downy serviceberry (*Amelanchier canadensis*): Really more like a tree, downy serviceberry is gorgeous in spring, when it is covered in white flowers. Fruits in early summer are edible, like blueberries that have lost their tartness. Leaves turn papery orange and glow in fall. It grows 15 to 20 feet (4.5–6 m). Sun; regular to moist soil.

Buttonbush (*Cephalanthus occidentalis*): I'm not sure whether the name refers to the flower, the fruit or the whole effect of this roundish spreading shrub. Small, white fuzzy flowers appear in little round balls in midsummer, fruit (hard, brown round balls) in late summer. It grows 9 to 12 feet (2.7–3.7 m). Sun; moist soil.

Sweet pepperbush, a.k.a. summersweet (*Clethra alnifolia*): Offering a change from spring-flowering shrubs, sweet pepperbush produces spires of white, sweet-smelling flowers in mid- to late summer. Leaves turn an attractive yellow in fall. It grows 3 to 6 feet (1–2 m), sometimes taller. Open shade; moist acidic soil.

Red-osier dogwood (*Cornus stolonifera*, a.k.a. *C. sericea*): A shrub of interest in every season, red-osier dogwood is covered with clusters of white flowers in late spring/ early summer, bluish berries in late summer and striking red twigs in winter. It grows 4 to 8 feet (1.2–2.5 m). Flowering dogwood (*C. florida*), a small tree, is another good choice, with white flowers and dark leaves that turn scarlet in fall. Sun to open shade; prefers moist soil but will do fine in regular conditions.

Witch hazel (*Hamamelis virginiana*): There *is* something magical about this shrub. It blooms in late fall with bewitching and twisting yellow ribbonlike flowers that enliven the autumn and winter garden. Foliage is bright yellow in fall. It grows 8 to 15 feet (2.5–4.5 m). Sun to shade; moist to dry soil.

Oak-leaf hydrangea (*Hydrangea quercifolia*): The foliage of oak-leaf hydrangea is very attractive – large and, yes, oak-leaf-like, turning brownish red in fall. White flowers appear in late spring to early summer. It grows 4 to 6 feet (1.2–2 m). Sun to open shade; regular soil.

Winterberry (*Ilex verticillata*): A holly, winterberry is prized for its shiny leaves and bright red autumn berries, which are great for birds. (You'll need a male and a female plant to get berries.) Small flowers are whitish green and appear in late spring. It grows 4 to 6 feet (1.2–2 m), sometimes taller. Sun to part shade; moist to regular acidic soil.

Creeping juniper (*Juniperus horizontalis*): An evergreen shrub that creeps along the ground, juniper produces blue berries in summer. Sun; well-drained soil.

Bayberry (*Myrica pensylvanica*): The fragrant leaves of this shrub make a deliciously soothing tea. Flowers are small, grayish white catkins. Leaves turn bronzish in fall. It grows 4 to 6 feet (1.2–2 m). Sun to part shade; moist to dry, sandy soil.

Wild rose, a.k.a. Virginia rose (*Rosa virginiana*): More understated than its cultivated cousins, but certainly of great beauty, the wild rose has pale pink flowers in summer and attractive hips in fall. Leaves are dark green. It grows 6 to 8 feet (2–2.5 m). Sun; moist to dry soil.

Highbush blueberry (*Vaccinium corymbosum*): With its twisted branches, dense clusters of white flowers in late spring and edible berries in summer, highbush blueberry is a good choice for the garden. It grows to approximately 6 feet (2 m). Sun to part shade; moist acidic soil.

Nannyberry, a.k.a. sweet viburnum (*Viburnum lentago*): Another shrub of interest in many seasons, nannyberry produces sweet-smelling clusters of creamy white flowers in early summer. Its dark foliage turns bright red in fall, and its berries are dark blue and appear in late summer. It grows 10 to 15 feet (3–4.5 m). Sun to shade; moist to regular soil; very adaptable.

In many areas of the mid-Atlantic, such as here at New Canaan Nature Center in Connecticut, rocks are a fact of gardening life and can be used to advantage in the garden's design – to line paths, for example.

5 PLANNING AND PLANTING

THE NUTS AND BOLTS

*"Plants neither author nor read gardening books.
The best sources of advice are the plants themselves."*

– Mike McKeag, posting on Internet discussion group <pnwnatives@cornetto.chem.washington.edu>, December 29, 1996

SINCE NATIVE-PLANT gardening is based on mimicking indigenous plant communities, there's no better place for the native-plant gardener to start than by looking at local native-plant communities in the wild. Meander in meadows, feel the forest, root around (figuratively, not literally) in riparian areas, ponder the prairies, soak up the savanna's specialness – in short, experience native plants in their natural habitats. Notice the ways in which particular species seem to cluster together or the fact that certain plants are never associated. Perhaps one species repels another. Perhaps one species supports another, either through some unseen symbiotic chemical association or literally, as structural support.

This is the information that will lead to native-plant gardening success, and it is information best learned through close contact. Join naturalist-group outings to wild areas, or simply explore on your own with a good field guide, but go to the *source* – the remaining wilderness areas in your region.

Close contact also best describes the kind of relationship you should have with your specific plot. After discovering the native habitats in your particular region, after seeing the typical flora and the ways these plants grow, your gardening task is one of translation: adapting the grammar and structure of nature to your garden's reality.

Questions you'll need to ask and answer include those familiar to any kind of gardening endeavor. What is the soil like? Is it sandy, gravelly, coarse, loamy, clayey? Is it of uniform texture and composition, or does it vary throughout the garden? What is the soil's pH? Is the soil nutrient-rich or nutrient-poor or somewhere in between? What is the drainage like? What is the nature of the sunlight that your garden receives? Bright morning sun, then dappled shade for the rest of the day, deep shade throughout, blazing sun all day or light shade? How moist

This garden captures the mood of a northwestern forest but is imbued with a sense of purposeful design.

Previous spread: If you plan your garden well, you'll have plenty of time to sit back and enjoy your creation.

PLANNING CHECKLIST: THE SPECIFICS OF YOUR GARDEN

LIGHT CONDITIONS

sun
partial sun
shade
exposure: north, south, east, west

SOIL

texture
acidity or alkalinity (pH)
fertility
drainage

CLIMATE

rainfall patterns
prevailing winds
cold- and warm-air patterns

TOPOGRAPHY

variation in grade
erosion patterns

or dry is the soil? Does it vary dramatically depending on the season? Is the terrain varied? Is it uniformly flat, or are there slopes and dips? Are some places prone to erosion? How does the wind flow through your landscape? Do buildings or trees create wind tunnels? It's necessary to know these site-specific details in order to match plants and plant communities to your plot.

Prairie Gardens

Prairie Preparation and Planting*

It is both a blessing and a curse that so much research is being done on what makes prairies tick: a blessing because the prairie gardener has hundreds of fine references available; a curse because such information rapidly becomes overwhelming, is often of use only in specific contexts and conditions and can at times be downright contradictory. The best approach is to look to certain key prairie principles for guidance but to learn by doing; in other words, be prepared to experiment and be adaptable.

As with any kind of native-plant gardening, you must first evaluate your own conditions and explore the local native habitat on which you plan to model your garden (see above). As well, you should talk with prairie gardeners and prairie experts at nurseries in your area, as the techniques that follow are general guidelines only, and there may be significant variations for your specific site.

The main requirement of a prairie garden is sunlight – lots of it, at least six hours a day. But the prairie garden is also one of the most forgiving in terms of soil requirements. I've seen gorgeous prairies on clay soil, on sand and on everything in between. Rather than going to great lengths to rework the soil, most prairie gardeners match the plants with the soil conditions at hand (see the plant lists in Chapter 3). However, if the soil is heavy clay or sand, adding organic materials such as compost will improve drainage and texture.

*The techniques to establish a meadow garden are virtually the same as those for a prairie garden.

If you get all worked up about soil fertility in the prairie garden and add too much in the way of soil amendments prior to planting, you may actually be doing your plants a disservice. A highly fertile bed, especially in the early days of your prairie garden's life, offers a leg up for weeds – something you definitely want to avoid, for weeds are *the* bane of the prairie garden. So while soil amendments are probably not in order, preparing a weed-free soil bed most certainly *is*.

John Morgan, a prairie expert in western Canada who established the Prairie Habitats nursery in Argyle, Manitoba, offers a cautionary analogy that points to the importance of preparing a weed-free soil bed. He compares two houses that look identical, but one was built *with* a foundation and the other without. Obviously, the house with the proper foundation is going to last longer and be more structurally sound. Think of a weed-free soil bed as your garden's foundation.

You can create this weed-free soil bed in a number of ways, depending on the size of your garden and the nature of the existing plants. Let's say, for example, that your future prairie garden is now lawn. Don't trust anyone who says that all you need to do is to scatter prairie seeds in the lawn, then sit back and enjoy. Unfortunately, this verging-on-effortless method is *not* an option. Your prairie seeds won't stand a chance against lawn turf; few seeds will even germinate. Nope, work is required.

While scattering seed in the lawn won't work, some people have had success planting seedlings of prairie forbs and grasses in the lawn, creating, in effect, little islands of prairie plants that will, the theory goes, expand and eventually take over. I would urge caution with this method. While it may work over the long term, it is slower, as you're making it more difficult for the prairie plants to become established, forced as they are to compete with the bullies of the school ground, the turf grasses. (This is especially true in the northern prairie regions and in areas with high rainfall.)

Much better to accept the inevitable right from the beginning – and turf the turf. Dig it up manually if the amount of coverage is not too daunting (a sod-slicing tool is deeply satisfying); if necessary, resort to mechanical means. If, for example, you're dealing with a large plot and manual cultivation is not an option, consider spending at least one entire growing season on mechanical cultivation, first plowing, then shallow-disking or cultivating every two weeks.

Yes, this involves delayed gratification, but the relatively weed-free results more than make up for it.

Or consider solarizing the planting bed by covering it with clear or black plastic (anchored with rocks) for six to eight weeks. This method has the advantage of not disturbing the soil, though it may kill some beneficial soil organisms. However, this may be a small – and temporary – price to pay for the effectiveness of total weed annihilation, which solarization is good at.

I should note, of course, that some people may be tempted to resort to chemical means. Consider all the underground life you would be killing too, along with the insects and birds you would be affecting, the groundwater pollution, and on and on. However, some prairie experts warn that in northern prairie regions or on highly fertile soil, a glyphosate herbicide such as Roundup™, which breaks down rapidly in the soil, may be necessary to eradicate weeds from large planting areas.

Once you've removed the turf (and if you're wondering what to do with it, Annette Alexander of Milwaukee suggests that you use some inverted clumps as mulch for your young prairie plants), however, all is not clear sailing. Lurking in the soil, ready to explode into prolific production, are untold millions (no exaggeration) of weed seeds. Denizens of disturbance, these weed seeds will see your backbreaking efforts as oh-so-kind preparation for *their* star turn on stage, not, as you have imagined, for your prairie planting. So a sneaky trick is in order, something to fool those seeds into germinating so that you can then heartlessly nip them in the bud.

Water the bed, urge those weeds on, and in a few days, after they've germinated, cruelly turn them under or pull them out. If you have the strength and the patience, repeat the process. The more you do now to eradicate weeds, the more leisure time you'll have later.

Another option for turf-grass eradication, and one that does not require a lot of digging, involves covering the lawn with several layers of newspaper – about 10 sheets thick. Then you'll need a delivery of soil – enough to cover to a depth of at least 6 inches (15 cm). Make sure, of course, that your source guarantees a weed-free batch of soil. I've heard countless stories of frustrating sproutings coming from expensive deliveries; unfortunately, you may be importing next year's headache in all that rich triple-mix. Instead of soil, though, you can use a mixture of sand and leaf mold.

When planning your prairie garden, consider the needs of wildlife too – by planting larval food and nectar sources for butterflies and by putting up birdhouses and leaving old snags for birds.

When you've prepared the seed bed and mapped out any paths, you're ready to plant. For prairie gardens, there are two camps of opinion: one says plant in spring (or early summer, depending on where you are); the other says plant in late fall. Obviously, both work. And there are benefits and drawbacks to both. A spring planting gives your seeds and/or seedlings one season's worth of growth before the plants have to cope with winter. The weeds, though, will be sprouting away too, and it will be difficult in the early days to tell them apart from desirable plants. If you plant in the late fall, chances are that most of the plants which sprout early the next spring will be weeds. (As a rule, prairie plants are warm-season species, which means that they really don't get going until the soil warms up.) You'll therefore be able to do more weeding before your prairie plants appear.

Many sources also recommend late-fall planting in heavy clay or sandy soil, because the soil will be at its moistest (though some sources report more of a weed problem when seeds are planted in clay soil in fall). As well, fall planting of seeds ensures that the seeds go through a natural stratification period (their cold-weather dormancy, which they require before they'll sprout). However, this should be done in late fall to ensure that the seeds don't germinate before winter. If you plant seeds in spring, either put the seeds through an artificial stratification process (see page 139) or make sure that the nursery has stratified them.

Another choice is between seeds and seedlings. Your decision will depend on the size of your prairie planting, your budget and your patience quota. (Can you wait the three years, on average, that it will take for seeds to bloom?) If you're planting a large area, seeds may be the only realistic option. However, if you're planting a typical urban or suburban lot, you may choose to use seedlings or, if your budget doesn't allow for that, a mix of seeds and seedlings. Many prairie gardeners opt for a mix: using seedlings of forbs, placed about a foot apart, and seeds of grasses.

If you choose seeds, plant some labeled pots with each species you broadcast in the prepared bed. Then you will have something to compare your sprouts to and will be able to distinguish your plants from weed sprouts. There's little worse than the indecision that arises when you are confronted with all those sprouts and have nothing to guide you in your weeding efforts.

To plant seed on a prepared bed, simply mix about half of your seed with

three parts sand or vermiculite and walk in one direction, broadcasting the
seed as you go. Then mix the rest of the seed with sand or vermiculite, and
walk at a right angle to your original direction. The amount of seed you need
depends on the species' germination rate, the quality of the seed, the proportion of grasses to forbs, etc. However, a rough guideline is that you should
have a ratio of about 60:40 or 50:50 of forbs to grasses by weight. On one
acre (0.4 ha), this would work out to roughly 14 to 20 pounds (6–9 kg) of forb
seed and 7 to 10 pounds (3–4.5 kg) of grass seed; or about one ounce (28 g) of
seed per 100 square feet (9.3 m²). It's best to consult your nursery source to
discuss your needs, as there are other factors to consider, such as soil type and
method of planting.

After broadcasting the seed, rake the bed lightly, roll it so that there's good
soil-seed contact, then water. You might want to mulch at this stage to conserve
moisture, using a light cover of weed-free straw, particularly on sandy or clay
soils. The important thing is to keep the bed well watered throughout the first
growing season.

Don't be alarmed if there is relatively little aboveground growth during the
first growing season. Remember that prairie plants are able to withstand the
rigors of prairie conditions precisely because of their deep, extensive root systems – and this is what the plants will be developing during the first season.

Unfortunately, though, while doing all this good work *below* the soil, your
prairie plants will be subject to intense weed competition at the surface. It's
better to cut rather than pull these weeds. Pulling will disturb the soil, invite
new invasions and possibly disrupt tiny prairie seedlings. Indeed, many prairie
gardeners recommend mowing the planting to about 5 to 8 inches (13–20 cm)
during the first growing season, or before weeds go to seed. Mowing won't
harm your prairie plants (prairie grasses, for example, grow from the base of
the stem, not the tip), and it will help to control weeds.

Rather than using signature prairie
plants in a conventional design (in ornamental clumps, for example), this
prairie garden closely mimics the feel of
a wild prairie.

PRAIRIE MAINTENANCE

While visiting the world's oldest restored prairie – the Curtis Prairie at the
University of Wisconsin-Madison Arboretum – I bought an unlikely postcard.
It shows flames burning tall (about 10 feet/3 m or so), scorched earth and a

fellow adding fuel, in the form of dried grasses, to the inferno – such an unusual image to celebrate for those of us raised on Smokey the Bear. But not for those researching prairie restoration, for in the past few decades, word has spread that fires and prairies go hand in hand.

In the days before European settlement, prairie fires were a regular occurrence. Not only did the native peoples start them deliberately, but lightning strikes also ignited miles and miles of prairie vegetation, sweeping across huge expanses. But far from being a destructive force, fires played a crucial role in the prairie ecosystem. They kept out non-fire-adapted woody species that would otherwise, in the inexorable march of succession, take over the prairie and turn it into woodland rather than grassland; they immolated accumulated ground litter, returning nutrients rapidly and efficiently to the soil in the form of ash; and they warmed up the soil, giving the warm-season prairie species an extra push.

But with settlement came fire suppression. The ecological cost of removing an essential element from the prairie ecosystem can be seen in prairie after prairie. Woody and exotic species are taking hold, and prairie species are losing vigor in the absence of rejuvenating flames. (All this may explain why some prairie enthusiasts often sound like closet pyromaniacs. I know of one fellow who, after a relaxing drink or two, waxes dreamily about "accidentally" dropping a match on a small patch of degraded urban prairie savanna in Toronto, Ontario. He knows that even one fire would start the process of prairie rejuvenation, though he also knows that city officials would be down on him like a ton of bricks – fires and cities being uncomfortable companions.)

On the other hand, hundreds of urban backyard prairie gardeners *have* gone the official route, calming nervous neighbors, enlisting the local fire department, registering for permits and conducting prairie burns in their urban environments. Such a commitment, however, takes time, patience, knowledge and a herd of helpers. It is not for the novice. Or, as the ads say, do not try this at home – unless you've done all the background work *first*.

Let's say, for example, that your young prairie is two or three years old. Ecologically, a controlled burn is entirely in order, particularly as a mechanism to fight exotic weeds. You'll need to ensure that there are firebreaks, such as gravel paths or mowed areas, which will serve as protective barriers preventing the fire's spread into surrounding areas. If you're in the United States, you must apply to the Environmental Protection Agency for a burn permit; if you're in Canada, apply to the provincial Ministry of Natural Resources. After this permit has been secured, you'll have to contact your local fire department and follow its process of application for a controlled burn. And, obviously, you should let your neighbors know of your plans. (I've heard of one prairie burn that was derailed when the fire trucks supervising the burn were called away because someone a mile away had reported smoke – the very smoke resulting from the deliberate burn.)

There's a lot more to it than permits, of course. As with any restoration activity, there's an art and a science to a burn: understanding wind patterns, knowing how fires behave, knowing how *people* behave at the sight of flames roaring and rushing with great intensity (although, in fact, some prairie burns can be disappointingly subdued affairs for the pyros in the crowd – just fluttering little poofs that are over in minutes). For anyone seriously considering a prairie burn, a very useful source is Wayne Pauly's booklet *How to Manage Small Prairie Fires* (available at a small cost from the Dane County Park Commission, 4318 Robertson Road, Madison, Wisconsin 53714). And it's a good idea to hook up with other prairie gardeners who have been involved in a burn (see the prairie source list at the end of the book).

If all this sounds like too much work – or if you're not up to convincing neighbors of the safety of your plan – there are many other options for maintaining a prairie garden. For example, if the idea of a fire appeals but you want something a little more controlled, you can mimic the effects of a burn by mowing your prairie garden in midspring, taking all the clippings to a fire pit, then having a kind of ceremonial burn. (Investigate permit requirements first, of course. Even this kind of open burning is not allowed in many places.) Afterward, you can spread the ashes on the garden.

Or you can bypass fire altogether and just mow or scythe. Midspring is the recommended time, but you can also mow in midfall. Or experiment with mowing sections of your prairie at different times of the year – grasses and wildflowers will respond in different ways to various mowing regimes, as will wildlife. (Ground-nesting birds, for example, may be adversely affected by a late-spring mowing, as this is when they're building their nests.) There's no "one size fits all" rule in this, so experiment, talk with other gardeners and observe what your prairie garden is telling you.

When your prairie garden is established, a mowing once a year to about

6 inches (15 cm) or a burn every few years, along with regular weed patrols, will be about the only maintenance required. In other words, prairie gardens eventually need little effort – but only after a few years of much effort.

Woodlands

If I were forced to characterize the stereotypical gardener's response to shady conditions, I'd say that it runs the gamut from arboreal ambivalence to outright tree trashing. Trained to evaluate garden success with a Mediterranean eye, many of us view shade as an obstacle to the sunny, colorful splashes we'd like to create. Happily, though (and not a moment too soon, given global warming, habitat loss, and so on), North America seems to have been gripped by forest fervor in the past decade. Not only are we offered opportunities to donate to tree-planting efforts in far-flung places, but we can't visit a fast-food restaurant on Earth Day without heading home with a spindly seedling. To our credit, we've embraced tree planting with open arms.

On the down side, however, I'm worried about the long-term success rate of all those spindly seedlings handed out by the thousands in spring. The problem isn't that they're spindly (in my lexicon, spindly is a gesture of optimism to the future); rather, it's that without proper soil preparation and aftercare, tree seedlings will often die. There's no getting around the essential fact of woodlands: they are not instant habitats. They develop slowly (at times, it seems, glacially); they demand the proper soil conditions, and in the early years, they don't put on a splashy show. In other words, they take time. (Four years later, and I still need to wear my future-vision goggles when surveying my small woodland plot. The dreams are pretty, the reality patchy, though each year less so.)

If you're creating a woodland garden, get ready for a rewarding but lengthy lesson in patience. Indeed, you'll be happiest if you learn to think like a tree: setting down sturdy roots (the soil prep), manufacturing your own food (the leaf mold and compost additions to the soil) and committing to the long term (the five or so years it takes to get established). You're in it for the long haul.

And the place to start is, as it is in the forest, with the soil. In the woodland garden, the key to all else is healthy, rich, humusy, good earth, and this means compost, lots of it. I've yet to meet a gardener who can possibly make too much of the stuff or add it too liberally to the woodland garden. Compost is a garden drug without overdose potential. Every woodland garden needs a bin or heap or pile. But failing that, or in addition to it, you need leaves. Dead leaves by the bagful. Or leaf mulch or wood chips or shredded bark – basically, organic materials to enrich the soil.

If you're adding woody waste (such as wood chips) to the soil, it will temporarily rob the soil of nitrogen. So add some manure too – another potent drug in the woodland gardener's little black bag.

You need to continue your soil-building activities throughout the life of the garden, enriching the soil with compost and leaf mulch every season. Think of it as the slow but steady accumulation and accretion of fuel, something like the body's demands for life. Sure, a big breakfast will take you far, but you'll crash without more nutrients. The woodland garden is the same. Keep it well fed.

Also, because many of the woodland communities in the eastern regions of the continent are relatively rich in rainfall throughout the growing season (and in the Northwest, rich in rainfall in the spring and fall, though often droughty in the summer months), your native woodland garden will be particularly successful if you take steps to maximize moisture retention. Mulch plants, for example, with topdressings of compost and leaf mold to help retain moisture in the soil, keep plants healthier and lessen weed problems. In the winter, of course, in the northeastern regions, snow provides the ideal mulch. Pile it on (as long as the snow is not contaminated with salt, that is).

In the northwestern regions of the continent, remember that the native woodland soils, while not as deep and duffy as the woodland soils in the northeastern regions, are typically more acidic, because of the acidifying detritus of conifers, such as needles. Thus chances are that your soil will already have a relatively low pH (i.e., it will be acidic), and you should endeavor to keep it that way, as many of the northwestern woodland natives are adapted to acidic conditions. Conifer-needle mulches are ideal in this regard.

In northeastern woodlands, too, conditions tend to be slightly more acidic than neutral. However, many native plants for the northeastern woodland garden will do just fine in neutral to slightly acidic soil.

Dense plantings in the woodland garden will ensure that weeds don't become a problem. Here, dentaria, bellwort, Virginia bluebells and trilliums carpet the ground.

If you're starting your woodland garden from scratch (if, for example, you have some trees but no native perennials), put in seedlings at first. Then your woodland will be well on its way to filling in before you start experimenting with seed propagation. It's not that all woodland natives are difficult to start from seed (though some, such as trilliums, tend to be); rather, it's that some of them will take a long time to reach blooming growth (an average of five to seven years for trilliums, for instance). It's up to you, of course, but if you're interested in having a showy woodland as quickly as possible, the seedling route makes the most sense.

Once you've planted your native woodlanders, there are a number of maintenance practices to follow. Plants should be kept well watered for the first growing season, as they get established, because most native woodland plants (especially in the Northeast) are not adapted to drought. Mulch around new transplants to help retain moisture. Succulent young transplants are also most susceptible to pest attack, so keep an eye out for slugs and other nibblers.

But other than these regular maintenance practices (and regular soil-enriching), woodland gardens tend to be relatively carefree environments once established. And when groundcovers have carpeted the woodland garden floor, chances are that you'll have very few weeding chores.

While visiting the Wilton, Connecticut, garden club's display gardens at the Old Town Hall, I met Judy Quattrochi, one of the animating forces behind the native-plant and wildflower gardens. She introduced me to an ingenious method she uses to encourage people to plant natives in their gardens – she simply points to the wonderful combinations that are possible with familiar exotics and easy-to-grow natives.

In the Grotto Garden, for example, she plants natives with nonnatives in such a way that the native plant enhances the beauty of the nonnative and vice versa. A combination of native columbine and exotic epimedium, for instance, is a subtle triumph of shimmering red, the columbine flowers echoing the red edges of the newly emerging epimedium leaves. Judy also exploits the design possibilities of bold contrasts. The yellow of exotic lady's mantle, for example, comes to life beside native wild blue phlox and lavender-pink penstemon (*Penstemon smallii*). In yet another slyly persuasive maneuver, Judy looks for native replacements for common exotics – and it's hard to argue with the evidence before one's eyes. Why *not* replace the ever present exotic hosta with the comparable native, wild ginger?

Seed Collecting and Propagation

When I first started gardening, I speculated that I was so drawn to the activity because I needed to learn patience. My green thumb was trying to teach me something about my fickle one-season attention span. Soon enough, I realized that starting plants from seed was the surest way to retune my speedy pace to nature's rhythm.

Seed-starting rapidly becomes an obsession in its own right. There's something very satisfying about taking the tiniest bundle of genetic information and watching it grow into something so changed in form. The medieval alchemists had it right: mysterious change deserves awe and respect...and tinkering.

Sometimes, too, native plants just aren't available in the nursery trade as seedlings. You have to hunt them down through native-plant-society seed exchanges, sharing with other gardeners, or find seed sources in the wild (see "The Wild Collection of Native Plants and Seeds: Ethical Considerations" on page 141).

The wild is also the place to find all the information you need in order to ensure seed-starting success. Think of *when* a plant produces its seed. If it's in the fall, then you'll know that the seed has to go through some kind of cold-dormancy period (as it does in nature – with winter) before it will sprout. If, on the other hand, the plant produces seed in early summer, like columbine, you'll know that this cold-dormancy period is not necessary. The trick, of course, is to reproduce the conditions that cause seeds to germinate in the absence of gardeners.

For the vast majority of natives that require a cold-dormancy period, you have to do something called stratifying the seed. You can do this as nature does it by planting seeds in the fall (either in beds or in pots), or you can mimic nature's cold-dormancy period by storing seeds in the refrigerator for a length of time (usually around six weeks) and then potting them up.

In addition, some plants, for example legumes with hard seed coats, will benefit from scarification: breaking the tough seed coat with a small cut or scraping it with sandpaper before stratifying the seed. Other plants will do better with moist stratification: placing them in the refrigerator in a bag with moist sand. As well, the length of time that seeds should be stratified varies among species.

In my experience, though, one need not be tied to an exacting calendar. If you mimic the cold-dormancy period found in nature, most seeds will be fine.

Some prairie legumes, such as leadplant, wild lupine and Canada milk vetch, will germinate only if specific bacteria are present in the soil, so you may need to purchase the appropriate inoculant at a nursery.

RESOURCES ON PROPAGATION

There are a number of excellent resources for gardeners who want to start native plants from seed or to experiment with other propagation techniques such as cutting and layering. Useful sources include: *Collecting, Processing, and Germinating Seeds of Wildland Plants* by James A. Young and Cheryl G. Young (Portland: Timber Press, 1986), *Directory to Resources on Wildflower Propagation* by Gene A. Sullivan and Richard H. Daley (St. Louis, Missouri: National Council of State Garden Clubs and Missouri Botanical Garden, 1981), *Garden in the Woods Cultivation Guide* by William E. Brumbrack and David L. Longland (Framingham, Massachusetts: New England Wild Flower Society, 1986), *A Garden of Wildflowers* by Henry W. Art (Pownal, Vermont: Storey, 1986), *Gardening with Native Plants of the Pacific Northwest* by Arthur R. Kruckeberg (Seattle: University of Washington Press, 1996), *Growing and Propagating Wild Flowers* by Harry R. Phillips (Chapel Hill, North Carolina: University of North Carolina Press,

1985), *Growing Wildflowers: A Gardener's Guide* by Maria Sperka (New York: Charles Scribner's Sons, 1973), *The Native Garden: Propagating and Wildcrafting Native Plants* by David Howarth and Kahlee Keane (Alvena, Saskatchewan: Root Woman and Dave, 1995), *The Native Plant Primer* by Carole Ottesen (New York: Harmony Books, 1995), *The Prairie Garden* by J. Robert Smith and Beatrice S. Smith (Madison, Wisconsin: University of Wisconsin Press, 1980), *Prairie Propagation Handbook* by Harold Rock (Hales Corners, Wisconsin: Wehr Nature Center, 1974), *Restoring the Tallgrass Prairie* by Shirley Shirley (Iowa City: University of Iowa Press, 1994), *Wildflower Meadow Book* by Laura C. Martin (Charlotte, North Carolina: East Wood, 1986), *Wildflower Propagation Tips* by Margaret M. Marchi (Woodstock, Illinois: McHenry County Defenders, 1992) and *Wildflowers in Your Garden* by Viki Ferreniea (New York: Random House, 1993).

The Wild Collection of Native Plants and Seeds: Ethical Considerations

ANY DISCUSSION OF collecting seeds in the wild opens up a much larger question regarding the ethics of collection. As any gardener concerned with conservation issues knows, our efforts would be a profound failure if the promotion of native-plant gardening led to the depletion of wild-plant populations. Thus a number of general guidelines have been developed by native-plant societies and others involved with habitat issues.

Although the specifics of the guidelines may vary from one group to another, the main principle can be summed up with a very simple statement: Do not engage in collection activities that adversely affect the ability of wild native-plant populations to sustain themselves. If you're collecting seeds, for example, take no more than 10 percent of a plant's seed production, and even then, take seeds only if the plant population is large and abundant (more than 100 plants). Do not take *any* seeds from a plant that is locally or nationally rare.

Gardeners should buy trilliums (shown here with false Solomon's seal) from nurseries which guarantee that plants are nursery-propagated rather than pillaged from the wild.

Transplanting native plants from the wild into the garden is generally considered to be a very bad idea, unless there are extenuating circumstances. If the wild-plant population is in imminent danger of being destroyed for some other reason, such as development, then transplanting or attempting to save the plants through rescue is a useful (though uncertain) strategy. But in general, wild populations of native plants should be left exactly where they are – in the wild.

For the ethical gardener, then, plant sources will be nurseries, other gardeners and plant or seed exchanges. However, buying from the nursery trade does not automatically ensure guilt-free gardening; unfortunately, some nurseries get *their* plants from the wild. According to the New England Wild Flower Society, some of the native-plant species that are frequently collected from the wild and sold through nurseries include bird's-foot violet, black snakeroot, cardinal flower, Dutchman's breeches, ferns, hepatica, Jack-in-the-pulpit, lady's slipper, trillium, trout lily and Virginia bluebells.

The best way to be on guard against inadvertently supporting the wild collection of plants through nursery purchases is to ask the nurseries whether their native plants are nursery-propagated. If they can't answer in the affirmative and assure you that they raise their native plants from seed (i.e., that their plants are indeed nursery-propagated), then forgo the purchase and, instead, patronize a nursery that *can* make this guarantee. Perhaps the pressure of the marketplace (and the continued lobbying of native-plant groups) will help to rid the nursery trade of unethical collection practices.

For more information on the issue of wild-collected plants, contact the Canadian Wildflower Society, the New England Wild Flower Society or the National Wildflower Research Center (see the Sources section at the end of the book). An excellent book on the subject is *The Gardener's Guide to Plant Conservation* by Nina T. Marshall (Washington: World Wildlife Fund and the Garden Club of America, 1993).

Endangered and Rare Plants

Estimates vary, but whichever expert's statistics one chooses, the story is depressingly the same: *hundreds* of native-plant species are at risk of extinction in North America. While native-plant gardening will not reverse this threat – since the plants are losing *wild* habitat – it is important for gardeners not to contribute to further losses. That is, do not dig plants from the wild unless the wild area is slated for imminent destruction; buy only from nurseries which guarantee that their plants are nursery-propagated; and support efforts to conserve, protect and restore North America's remaining wild areas.

For more information on endangered plants and habitats, contact the Center for Plant Conservation (Missouri Botanical Garden, P.O. Box 299, St. Louis, Missouri 63166), the Canadian Botanical Conservation Network (c/o Royal Botanical Gardens, 680 Plains Road West, Burlington, Ontario L7T 4H4), the World Wildlife Fund (90 Eglinton Avenue East, Suite 504, Toronto, Ontario M4P 2Z7), your state natural-heritage program, the federal U.S. Fish and Wildlife Service (Division of Endangered Species, 18th and C Streets NW, M.S. 400 ARLSQ, Washington, D.C. 20240) or your provincial Ministry of the Environment.

Design

WHILE I HAVE deep admiration for designers, I'm afraid that I have little patience for design lingo. Terms such as balance and harmony, which delight in effect, leave me cold as talk. Perhaps it's because such terms tend to wander off into a sunset of vagueness when you actually try to pin them down. For example, define balance or harmony in a way that can be translated by anyone into an in-the-dirt planting. Hard, isn't it? The definitions just tend to slide into other, equally unpindownable terms such as equilibrium, steadiness, pleasing, and so on.

This is not to deny that such things as harmony and balance exist. One look at the native woodland garden at Casa Loma in Toronto or the Bloedel Reserve in Washington State or the West Chicago Prairie in Illinois or the neighbor's successful garden down the street proves that the elusive goal is attainable. It's just that finding the cipher – the magical key to translating concepts into action – often *is* elusive.

The best way to find that cipher, though, is to head for the hills or prairie or woodland or wetland – or whichever of nature's models your garden design is based on. *That's* where you'll find a lot of what you need to know about what does and doesn't work. (Nature knows no graph paper, I like to tell myself whenever I'm feeling particularly design-challenged.) Soak up as much information about heights and combinations and plant associations and color effects, and so on – right at the source. After all, the native-plant garden is modeled on plant communities in the wild, so it makes perfect sense to take your cues from nature's design. Adapt, fudge and fiddle with such information as you see fit, but nothing, to my mind, beats the design inspiration and practical guidance to be found in the wild.

So, with apologies to all those wonderful garden-design writers who are doing valiant work to shape our design aesthetic and hone our vision, go wild... (and that includes mixing red and orange and purple if the combo appeals to *you* – the ultimate arbiter of taste in *your* garden).

Afterword

Sometimes I wonder whether there isn't a contradiction at the heart of gardening's pleasure. In the place where we celebrate solitude, where we find solace in being alone with our thoughts and the dirt, we are, in fact, deeply connected with the world around us (for some of us, perhaps more so than at any other time or during any other activity). In the garden, we are active participants, equal partners in the give and take of connection.

If there's one theme to this book, it is that while our connection with the earth may find a wonderful, healing expression in our native-plant gardens, the process doesn't stop there. Connection is intricate, not simply two-way; alliances forged lead outward to other connections, other alliances, other possibilities of communion. And, to my mind, the healing promise of native-plant gardening is that it encourages us to look at the landscapes around us in a new way. When we're deep in the dirt trying to bring a small patch of butterfly weed to flower, we may ask ourselves where other patches of butterfly weed might be. And increasingly in North America, simply asking such questions leads to associated issues of habitat health, endangered species and spaces and on and on in an alarming catalog of losses.

Awareness leads to action. Our native-plant gardens themselves are a first healing step, but the challenge is to take that healing vision, harness the restorative promise and extend it to the *whole* landscape of home, whether one conceives of that home as local, bioregional, continental or global – or, indeed, as all of these.

If gardening to save the world seems hopelessly naive or simply too great a weight for the solitary gardener to shoulder, look again at the accumulated wisdom of the gardeners and at the beauty of the gardens in this book. Each gardener has forged a healing connection with the land and nurtured local growth in such a way that it is revealed as possible for all of us. These gardeners don't necessarily have unusual resources – unless, of course, one views curiosity, spunk, creativity and willingness to experiment as unusual commodities. No, they've simply started with the conditions at hand, explored the local possibilities and worked from the ground up.

As Wallace Stegner wrote: "Wilderness can be a means of reassuring ourselves of our sanity as creatures, a part of the geography of hope." I would say that native-plant gardening fits into this idea as part of the geography of hope *in action*. Every gardener will interpret "wildness" or "wilderness" in his or her own way. For some, it may be the incorporation of a few wildflowers in an essentially exotic garden; for others, it may be the full restoration of a functioning native-plant community. The important thing is to connect with that wildness and to feel it as part of oneself, to feel as "at home" in the garden as the butterfly searching for nectar, the bird searching for seed, the earthworm turning the soil.

While walking in the woodland wildflower garden at Longwood Gardens in Pennsylvania, I overheard a couple talking as they gazed at the foamflower.

"We could put that beside the house," she said.

"You know what's funny," he said with a catch in his voice, the surprise of connection sneaking up on him. "I grew up with that in the woods beside my house."

A healing embrace of home and a sense of our place within it – that's where the path of native-plant gardening leads.

The healing power of the native-plant path extends outward to the *whole* landscape we call home.

Sources

General Sources

Wildflower Gardening

Although numerous books on wildflower gardening are available, a few stand out as excellent (see the following pages for sources in specific regions): *A Garden of Wildflowers: 101 Native Species and How to Grow Them* by Henry Art (Pownal, Vermont: Storey, 1986); *A Gardener's Encyclopedia of Wildflowers* by C. Colston Burrell (Emmaus, Pennsylvania: Rodale Press, 1997); *Growing and Propagating Wild Flowers* by Harry R. Phillips (Chapel Hill, North Carolina: University of North Carolina Press, 1985); *Growing Wildflowers: A Gardener's Guide* by Maria Sperka (New York: Charles Scribner's Sons, 1973); *The Native Plant Primer* by Carole Ottesen (New York: Harmony Books, 1995); *Wildflowers in Your Garden* by Viki Ferreniea (New York: Random House, 1993). As well, organizations such as the Canadian Wildflower Society, the National Wildflower Research Center and the New England Wild Flower Society have numerous excellent fact sheets available on growing native plants (see list of National Organizations).

Three books that address the wider issues of native-plant gardening with great insight and vision are *Noah's Garden: Restoring the Ecology of Our Own Back Yards* by Sara Stein (Boston: Houghton Mifflin, 1993); *Planting Noah's Garden: Further Adventures in Backyard Ecology* by Sara Stein (Boston: Houghton Mifflin, 1997); *Requiem for a Lawnmower (and Other Essays on Easy Gardening With Native Plants)* by Sally Wasowski (Dallas: Taylor, 1992).

For those who want to learn more about the philosophy and science of ecological restoration, good places to start include: *City Form and Natural Process* by Michael Hough (London: Routledge, 1989); *Helping Nature Heal: An Introduction to Environmental Restoration*, edited by Richard Nilsen (Berkeley: Ten Speed, 1991); *Landscape Restoration Handbook*, edited by Donald Harker et al. (Ann Arbor: Lewis Publishers, 1993); *Restoration Ecology: A Synthetic Approach to Ecological Research* by William R. Jordan III, Michael E. Gilpin and John D. Aber (New York: Cambridge University Press, 1987); *Restoring Nature's Place* by Jean-Marc Daigle and Donna Havinga (Schomberg, Ontario: Ecological Outlook Consulting and the Ontario Parks Association, 1996); *In Service of the Wild* by Stephanie Mills (Boston: Beacon Press, 1995).

Plant Communities and Native Plants in the Wild

General sources on the flora of North America include *Flora of North America North of Mexico*, edited by Nancy Morin (New York: Oxford University Press, 1993) and *The Flora of Canada* by H.J. Scoggan (Ottawa: National Museums of Canada, 1978).

As well, gardeners can contact university herbaria in their region or local field naturalist groups; many have published excellent guides to local flora.

Other references to wild-plant communities include: *Field and Forest: A Guide to Native Landscapes for Gardeners and Naturalists* by Jane Scott (New York: Walker & Co., 1984); *The Natural Vegetation of North America: An Introduction* by John L. Vankat (New York: Wiley, 1979); *The Plant Observer's Guidebook: A Field Botany Manual for the Amateur Naturalist* by Charles E. Roth (Englewood Cliffs, New Jersey: Prentice-Hall, 1984).

Gardening for Wildlife

Good places to start are: *The Backyard Naturalist* by Craig Tufts (Washington: National Wildlife Federation, 1988); *Butterflies: How to Identify Them and Attract Them to Your Garden* by Marcus Schneck (Emmaus, Pennsylvania: Rodale, 1990; *The Butterfly Book* by Donald and Lillian Stokes and Ernest Williams (Boston: Little, Brown, 1991); *Butterfly Gardening*, edited by L. Gunnarson and

F. Haselsteiner (San Francisco: The
Xerces Society/Smithsonian Institution,
Sierra Club, 1990); *A Complete Guide to
Bird Feeding* by John V. Dennis (New
York: Knopf, 1986); *The Hummingbird
Garden* by Mathew Tekulsky (New York:
Crown, 1990); *Trees, Shrubs and Vines for
Attracting Birds: A Manual for the Northeast*
by Richard M. Degraaf and Gretchin M.
Witman (Amherst: University of Massa-
chusetts Press, 1979); *Landscaping for
Wildlife* by Carrol Henderson (St. Paul,
Minnesota: Minnesota Department of
Natural Resources, 1987);*The Wildlife
Gardener* by John V. Dennis (New York:
Knopf, 1985).

National Organizations

Canadian Nature Federation, 1 Nicholas
Street, Suite 520, Ottawa, on k1n 7b7;
<http://www.magma.ca/~cnfgen>
Canadian Wildflower Society, P.O. Box
336, Station F, Toronto, Ontario m4y
2l7; <http://www.acornonline.com/
hedge/cws.htm>
Canadian Wildlife Federation, 2740
Queensview Drive, Ottawa, on k2b 1a2;
<http://www.cwf-fcf.org>
Center for Plant Conservation, P.O. Box
299, St. Louis, mo 63166; <http://
cisus.mobot.org/CPC/>
National Wildflower Research Center,
4201 La Crosse Avenue, Austin, tx
78739; <http://www.wildflower.org>
National Wildlife Federation, 1400-16th
Street nw, Washington, dc 20036-
2266; <http://www.nwf.org/nwf/
index.html>
New England Wild Flower Society, 180
Hemenway Road, Framingham, ma
01701-2699; <http://www.ultranet
.com/~newfs/newfs.html>

Society for Ecological Restoration, 1207
Seminole Highway, Suite B, Madison,
wi 53711; <http://nabalu.flas.ufl.edu/
ser/SERhome.html>

Magazines

Butterfly Gardeners' Quarterly (P.O. Box
30931, Seattle, Washington 98103).
Plant Talk (P.O. Box 65226, Tucson,
Arizona 35728-5226).
The Prairie Reader (P.O. Box 8227,
St. Paul, mn 55108).
Restoration Ecology, published by the
Society for Ecological Restoration
(available from Blackwell Scientific
Publications, 238 Main Street,
Cambridge, Massachusetts 02142,
or from the Society for Ecological
Restoration, 1207 Seminole Highway,
Suite B, Madison, Wisconsin 53711).
Restoration & Management Notes, pub-
lished by the University of Wisconsin
Press (114 North Murray Street,
Madison, Wisconsin 53715).
Wild Flower Notes, published by the New
England Wild Flower Society (180
Hemenway Road, Framingham,
Massachusetts 01701-2699).
Wildflower, published by the Canadian
Wildflower Society (P.O. Box 336,
Station F, Toronto, Ontario m4y 2l7).
Wild Garden (1421 Parker Street,
Springfield, Oregon 97477).

Sources for Northwestern Gardeners

Nurseries specializing in native plants exist throughout the Northwest. There's even a publication that lists them: *Hortus West: A Western North American Native Plant Directory & Journal* (published by Pacific Habitat Services, P.O. Box 2870, Wilsonville, OR 97070-2870); <http://www.teleport.com/~phabitat>.

Northwest Wildflower Gardening

The bible of native-plant gardening in the Northwest is Art Kruckeberg's book *Gardening with Native Plants of the Pacific Northwest* (Seattle, Washington: University of Washington Press, 2nd edition, 1996). Other resources include April Pettinger's *Native Plants in the Coastal Garden: A Guide for Gardeners in British Columbia and the Pacific Northwest* (Vancouver: Whitecap, 1996); Henry Art's *The Wildflower Gardener's Guide: Pacific Northwest, Rocky Mountain, and Western Canada Edition* (Pownal, Vermont: Garden Way, 1990); Donald and Lillian Stokes' *The Wildflower Book: From the Rockies West* (Toronto: Little, Brown and Co., 1993).

Wildlife Gardening

The following organizations all provide information on gardening with native plants. A terrific Web site can be found at <http://chemwww.chem.washington.edu/natives/>.

Naturescape British Columbia, 300–1005 Broad Street, Victoria, BC V8W 2A1

Washington Department of Fish and Wildlife, 16018 Mill Creek Boulevard, Mill Creek, WA 98012

The Oregon Department of Fish and Wildlife's Naturescaping Program, P.O. Box 59, Portland, OR 97207

National Wildlife Federation, Backyard Wildlife Habitat Program, Oregon Field Office, 921 SW Morrison Street, #512, Portland, OR 97205

Organizations

For communion with other native-plant gardeners – to share information and inspiration – join one of the very active native-plant societies in the Northwest, many of which also have local chapters.

Alaska   Alaska Native Plant Society, P.O. Box 141613, Anchorage, AK 99514–1613

British Columbia   Native Plant Society of British Columbia, 2012 William Street, Vancouver, BC V5L 2X6
Native Plant Study Group of the Victoria Horticultural Society, P.O. Box 5081, Station B, Victoria, BC V8R 6N3; <http://www.freenet.victoria.bc.ca/vic.hort/>

Colorado   Colorado Native Plant Society, P.O. Box 200, Fort Collins, CO 80522–0200

Montana   Montana Native Plant Society, P.O. Box 8783, Missoula, MT 59807–8782

Oregon   Native Plant Society of Oregon, P.O. Box 902, Eugene, OR 97440; <http://www.teleport.com/nonprofit/npso/>.

Washington   Washington Native Plant Society, P.O. Box 28690, Seattle, WA 98118–8690; <http://www.wnps.org>
The WNPS publishes the excellent journal *Douglasia* and maintains an E-mail discussion group for members only.

A spirited Internet discussion group well worth joining is <pnw-natives@cornetto.chem.washington.edu>.

Sources for Prairie Gardeners

For a list of native-plant nurseries specializing in prairie plants, contact the Wild Ones or the Alberta Native Plant Council (see following list of organizations).

Prairie Wildflower Gardening

Conservation of Canada's Prairie Grasslands: A Landowner's Guide by Garry C. Trottier (Edmonton: Supply and Services Canada, 1992); *The Native Garden: Propagating and Wildcrafting of Native Plants* by David Howarth and Kahlee Keane (Alvena, Saskatchewan: Root Woman and Dave, 1995); *The Prairie Garden: 70 Native Plants You Can Grow in Town or Country* by J. Robert Smith and Beatrice S. Smith (Madison: University of Wisconsin Press, 1980); *Prairie Propagation Handbook* by Harold Rock (Hales Corners, Wisconsin: Wehr Nature Center, 1974); *Prairie Restoration for the Beginner* by Robert Ahrenhoerster and Trelen Wilson (North Lake, Wisconsin: Prairie Seed Source, 1981); *Prairie Wildflowers: An Illustrated Manual of Species Suitable for Cultivation and Grassland Restoration* by R. Currah, A. Smreciu and M. Van Dyk (Edmonton: Friends of the Devonian Botanic Garden, University of Alberta, 1983); *Restoring Canada's Native Prairies: A Practical Manual* by John P. Morgan, Douglas R. Collicutt and Jacqueline D. Thompson (Argyle, Manitoba: Prairie Habitats, 1995); *Restoring the Tallgrass Prairie: An Illustrated Manual for Iowa and the Upper Midwest* by Shirley Shirley (Iowa City: University of Iowa Press, 1994); *The Tallgrass Restoration Handbook: For Prairies, Savannas and Woodlands*, edited by Stephen Packard and Cornelia F. Matel (Washington, DC: Island Press, 1996); *The Wildflower Gardener's Guide: Midwest, Great Plains, and Canadian Prairies Edition* by Henry W. Art (Pownal, Vermont: Storey Communications, 1991); *Wildflower Meadow Book* by Laura C. Martin (Charlotte, North Carolina: East Wood, 1986).

General Prairie Ecology

The classics of the prairie genre include: *Miracle Under the Oaks* by William K. Stevens (New York, Pocket Books, 1995); *The Perfection of the Morning* by Sharon Butala (Toronto, HarperCollins, 1994); *PrairyErth* by William Least Heat-Moon (Boston: Houghton Mifflin, 1991); *A Sand County Almanac* by Aldo Leopold (New York: Oxford University Press, 1989); *Siftings* by Jens Jensen (Baltimore: Johns Hopkins University Press, 1990); *The Wheatgrass Mechanism: Science and Imagination in the Western Canadian Landscape* by Don Gayton (Saskatoon: Fifth House, 1990); *Where the Sky Began: Land of the Tallgrass Prairie* by John Madson (Boston: Houghton Mifflin, 1982).

Other good introductions to prairie ecology include: *Grasslands* by Lauren Brown (New York: Knopf, 1985); *The History, Biology, Politics, and Promise of the American Prairie* by Richard Manning (New York: Viking Penguin, 1995); *Konza Prairie: A Tallgrass History* by O.J. Reichman (Lawrence, Kansas: University Press of Kansas, 1987); *Prairie Plants and their Environment* by John E. Weaver (Lincoln, Nebraska: University of Nebraska Press, 1968); *The Prairie World* by David Costello (New York: Thomas Y. Crowell, 1969); *Tallgrass Prairie: The Inland Sea* by Patricia Duncan (Kansas City: Lowell Press, 1978); *The True Prairie Ecosystem* by P.G. Risser et al. (Stroudsberg, Pennsylvania: Hutchinson Ross, 1981).

Organizations

For a list of provincial and state native-plant societies, contact the Canadian Wildflower Society, the National Wildflower Research Center (see page 147) or the Web site <http://www.wildflower.org>.

The following organizations are also good resources:

Alberta Native Plant Council, Garneau P.O. Box 52099, Edmonton, AB T6G 2T5

Grand Prairie Friends, P.O. Box 36, Urbana, IL 61801; <http://www.prairienet.org/community/clubs/gpf/homepage.html>

Iowa Prairie Network, P.O. Box 261, Cedar Falls, IA 50613–0261; <http://www.netins.net/showcase/bluestem/ipnapp.htm>

Missouri Prairie Foundation, P.O. Box 200, St. Louis, MO 65205; <http://www.moprairie.org/>

The Prairie Enthusiasts, 4192 Sleepy Hollow Trail, Boscobel, WI 53805; <http://www.prairie.presenter.com/>

Rural Lambton Stewardship Network, P.O. Box 1168, Chatham, ON N7M 5L8

The Wild Ones, P.O. Box 23576, Milwaukee, WI 53223–0576

SOURCES FOR NORTHEASTERN GARDENERS

For a list of native-plant nurseries in your area, contact the Canadian Wildflower Society or the New England Wild Flower Society (see page 147).

WILDFLOWER GARDENING

Many of the general wildflower gardening books listed on page 146 are heavily weighted in favor of the northeastern regions. Other sources include: *Ferns: Wild Things Make a Comeback in the Garden* by C. Colston Burrell (Brooklyn: Brooklyn Botanic Garden, 1994); *Garden in the Woods Cultivation Guide* by William E. Brumbrack and David L. Longland (Framingham, Massachusetts: New England Wild Flower Society, 1986); *Growing and Propagating Showy Native Woody Plants* by Richard E. Bir (Chapel Hill, North Carolina: University of North Carolina Press, 1992); *Growing Woodland Plants* by Clarence and Eleanor G. Birdseye (New York: Dover, 1972); *The Wildflower Gardener's Guide: Northeast, Mid-Atlantic, Great Lakes, and Eastern Canada Edition* by Henry W. Art (Pownal, Vermont: Storey, 1987).

ORGANIZATIONS

Connecticut Connecticut Botanical Society, 10 Hillside Circle, Storrs, Connecticut 06268; <http://www.vfr.com/cbs/>

District of Columbia Botanical Society of Washington, Department of Botany, NHB 166, Smithsonian Institution, Washington, DC 20560; <http://www.fred.net/kathy/bsw.html>

Maine Josselyn Botanical Society, P.O. Box 41, China, ME 04926

Maryland Maryland Native Plant Society, P.O. Box 4877, Silver Spring, MD 20914

Massachusetts New England Wild Flower Society, 180 Hemenway Road, Framingham, MA 01701–2699; <http://www. ultranet. com/~newfs/newfs.html>

New Jersey The Native Plant Society of New Jersey, P.O. Box 231, Cook College, New Brunswick, NJ 08903–0231

New York New York Flora Association, New York State Museum, 3132 CEC, Albany, NY 12230

Nova Scotia Nova Scotia Wild Flora Society, Nova Scotia Museum, 1747 Summer Street, Halifax, NS B3H 3A6

Pennsylvania Botanical Society of Western Pennsylvania, 401 Clearview Avenue, Pittsburgh, PA 15205
Pennsylvania Native Plant Society, P.O. Box 281, State College, Pennsylvania 16804–0281

Prince Edward Island Island Nature Trust, P.O. Box 265, Charlottetown, PEI C1A 7K4

Rhode Island Rhode Island Wild Plant Society, 12 Sanderson Road, Smithfield, RI 02917–2606

Vermont Vermont Botanical and Bird Clubs, Warren Road, Box 327, Eden, VT 05652

Virginia Virginia Native Plant Society, P.O. Box 844, Annandale, VA 22003–08440

West Virginia West Virginia Native Plant Society, P.O. Box 2755, Elkins, WV 26241